T0393681

CLASSIC COCKTAIL

REVIVAL

JENNIFER BRIAN

CLASSIC COCKTAIL

Revival

Photography by **Jessie Kriech-Higdon** *and* **Jennifer Brian**
Illustrations by **Michelle F. VanderHouwen**

UNIVERSITY PRESS OF KENTUCKY

Copyright © 2025
by The University Press of Kentucky

Scholarly publisher for the Commonwealth, serving
Bellarmine University, Berea College, Centre College
of Kentucky, Eastern Kentucky University, The
Filson Historical Society, Georgetown College,
Kentucky Historical Society, Kentucky State
University, Morehead State University, Murray State
University, Northern Kentucky University, Spalding
University, Transylvania University, University of
Kentucky, University of Louisville, University of
Pikeville, and Western Kentucky University.

Editorial and Sales Offices:
The University Press of Kentucky
663 South Limestone
Lexington, Kentucky 40508-4008
www.kentuckypress.com

Cataloging-in-Publication data available
from the Library of Congress

ISBN 978-1-9859-0292-3 (hardcover)
ISBN 978-1-9859-0294-7 (pdf)
ISBN 978-1-9859-0293-0 (epub)

Manufactured in Canada

Member of the Association of University Presses

To all the women in my life who have fanned my flame, held me up when I couldn't stand on my own, straightened my crown, and reminded me who I am all the times in my life when I forgot. Mother, sister, daughter, BFF, bad bitches, kimono instapot collective, ride-or-dies, divas—you know who you are. You are the beat of my heart, now and forever.

CONTENTS

SERMON ON THE MOUNT

We have all been there. You experience the rapture of a sublime cocktail at your favorite restaurant. You are out on date night or waiting for a friend and the bartender recommends a seasonal cocktail you have never heard of. You watch the bartender perform the ritual of the cocktail: pour, measure, ice, shake, strain, garnish—the movements a meditation. Your anticipation builds right along with the cocktail. It is delivered to you, garnished beautifully, in sparkling stemware. The deep color of the cocktail draws you in; the first whiff sends your senses spinning as you go down for a sip. With that first taste, you are undone. You have never experienced anything like it. Your eyes roll back in ecstasy as you take another sip to make sure you haven't imagined the experience. How did all these perfect flavors come together in one place? How is it possible that you never had a cocktail like this before? You must take a moment, unable to speak, unable to think about anything other than what you just tasted. Your body comes alive, feeling satisfied and excited, brand new and eternal in a single moment. The tone is set for the rest of the evening. Whatever comes next, you are excited to be a part of it, your senses wide open.

You leave the restaurant and long to re-create the experience of that cocktail at home but have no idea what it was. You can remember only the spirit, some random liqueur you never heard of, and lemon. Was it lemon juice? Lemon oil? Lemon peel? How much lemon? And what do you do with it? Is the cocktail shaken, stirred, built in the glass? The photo you took of the cocktail menu offers no guidance. So, off you go to the liquor store to try to find any of the ingredients. Oh, if only you could relive that moment of bliss, of peace, of utter joy when you tasted that cocktail! The light shone brighter than it had moments before. The conversation felt more connected, the food tasted better, and the evening sparkled a little bit brighter. You absolutely must re-create it!

I'm not sure there is anything more intimidating than standing in a liquor store with aisle after aisle filled with thousands of bottles of spirits and liqueurs. Where do you even start? You start walking up and down the aisles, lost in the wilderness of the spirits shop. When the clerk asks if you need help finding something, you try to describe the cocktail, try to explain how special it was. The clerk looks at you blankly and suggests that if you don't know the ingredients, perhaps a canned cocktail would work. You are heartbroken and frustrated. Why does this have to be such toil? At this point, it would be so much easier to open a beer or a bottle of wine. Is that what you want? Absolutely, emphatically it is not, but who has time for all this turmoil?

Rejoice and be glad, my friends. I am here to deliver you. I am here to testify that the world of amazing craft cocktails does not have to be overwhelming and intimidating. What was once a barren desert of a home bar can now be a land of milk and honey—or lavender and honey, as the case may be. I believe that three-ingredient cocktails can be accessible, delicious, and easy and can fit into anyone's lifestyle or skill level. That utterly perfect cocktail moment can be re-created again and again in your own home.

When I cofounded Make & Muddle years ago, it was about bringing back the revered cocktail hour from long ago. Resurrecting cocktail hour became an even greater

> ## "Oh, if only you could relive that moment of bliss, of peace, of utter joy when you tasted that cocktail!"

necessity when the COVID-19 pandemic hit in 2020 and we were all working from home. Our daily commute was now down the hall instead of across town, and there was no separation between work life and home life. As we spent so much more time at home, our bars expanded. Home cocktail enthusiasts became more willing to experiment and learn new cocktail techniques. Blessed are the working-from-home weary, for theirs is the perfect evening cocktail.

Behold the heralding clink of ice in glass at 5:00 p.m., the happy song of a cocktail shaker with spirits chilling inside, the offering of fellowship to friends and family. The transformation from our work selves to our true selves becomes seamless through the rituals of cocktail hour.

Classic cocktails are the foundation for almost every new cocktail that has been developed. Martinis, Old-Fashioneds, Manhattans, sours, Negronis, daiquiris, toddies, sangrias, and spritzes are the original tribes of the cocktail world. There are countless variations, but the originals were all simple, minimal-ingredient cocktails. Simple does not have to be plain.

I am an executive bourbon steward, caterer, and event planner, and the expanded recipes in this book were developed either during my career working behind the bar or creating signature cocktails for special events or to celebrate

afternoons on the porch or in front of a fire with friends. They were inspired by amazing evenings out at a restaurant where I had a seasonal cocktail that changed my life or when I experienced an evening so perfect I wanted a beverage that was worthy of it. The art of gathering is one I have been striving to perfect my entire life. I am not sure the Promised Land exists, but if it does, I know that mine will always involve friends and family, fine cocktails, and food. Those things need not be righteously complicated or fussy, only delicious and authentic.

Over the years, I witnessed the growing trend of having signature cocktails at events. It was a way to elevate and personalize a special day. Cocktails were becoming more sophisticated and delicious, which often meant ingredient-heavy labors of love that involved house-made syrups and tinctures, infused spirits, and exotic liqueurs. While this can certainly differentiate one establishment from another, it is virtually impossible for the amateur to re-create that level of sophistication. I saw a growing need for delicious, easy craft cocktail mixers that folks could use at home.

I also wanted the mixers to be as flexible as possible, moving from clear to brown spirits seamlessly. Versatility is a high priority for me. I do not need a single-use anything on my bar, whether spirit,

ingredient, or mixer. If it cannot transition from one spirit, mood, or season to the next, I won't invest in it. Resources are not eternal in anyone's home, and I believe that whatever you spend your time, energy, and money on should deliver.

In the early stages of Make & Muddle, we created kits that had home bar enthusiasts steeping their own ingredients. I quickly learned that this wasn't practical. Folks wanted to pour all those beautiful flavors out of a bottle. I have taken on the work of creating sophisticated flavor profiles and giving them new life in one bottle. I banish the mystery of mixing a delicious cocktail. Works of mercy abound, and you can now build a sophisticated, delicious, three-ingredient cocktail at home. That being said, if you like the challenge of making your own syrups, I provide some recipes here and walk you through the process.

Along with the ability to create craft cocktails in the comfort of home, you can also customize cocktails. Cocktails on a Tuesday evening look different from cocktails on a Friday evening. Mixing your own craft cocktail enables you to control every aspect of the drink, from how sweet or sour it is to how much alcohol to use. Low-alcohol and spirit-free cocktails are not available in many bars and restaurants unless you are having a seltzer or a beer. With Make & Muddle or homemade syrups,

> ## "Three-ingredient cocktails can be accessible, delicious, and easy and can fit into anyone's lifestyle or skill level."

you can control the ingredients without sacrificing any of the flavor.

My philosophy is that the tradition of heritage foods and aged spirits was meant to be shared and passed down generation to generation. We are the keepers of culture. Staying true to original ideas while updating methods is a necessity if we want those ideas to endure. Although the grain recipes (also called mash bills) of the best spirits in the world remain largely unchanged, the contemporary science of yeast strains has made flavor profiles more consistent. Similarly, while a classic Old-Fashioned still consists of spirit, sugar, water, and bitters, we can come out of the darkness and into the light and use a beautifully simple yet sophisticated syrup and a bourbon-soaked cherry garnish instead. No grainy, muddled fruit necessary. Welcome to the twenty-first century. Hallelujah, amen.

I also profess that a finished product is only as good as the ingredients in it, regardless of whether they come from your kitchen or elsewhere. This means high standards for quality and countless iterations of trial and error. Make & Muddle products are the result of decades of culinary and cocktail experience. Ingredients for the mixers, syrups, and shrubs are sourced from small growers and local companies whenever possible, ensuring the freshest ingredients available. Seasonal is my favorite way to cook as well as drink. Fresh ingredients harvested at the peak of the season are delicious and a joy to prepare. But there is also an indulgent elegance associated with drinking or eating out of season. Strawberry margaritas in January feel a little sinful, and sometimes we like that.

Enjoying fine cocktails made with thoughtful ingredients establishes a connection between those who create them and those who enjoy them. Make & Muddle products and the offerings from your own kitchen are an authentic expression of the belief that our time together makes life meaningful and centered.

As a self-proclaimed cocktail evangelist, I am here to bring you good news about booze. I hope to introduce new drinkers to my favorite spirits, as well as expand the libraries of tried-and-true cocktail fans. My message is one of hope and promise: you can cocktail. The classic cocktail revival is here, my brothers and sisters, and it is delicious.

Cheers Y'all

Jennifer

1

IN THE BEGINNING

A classically American drink, the original cocktail consisted of a distilled spirit, sugar, water, and bitters—which is still the basic recipe for the Old-Fashioned. But today a cocktail can be so many things that it's difficult to know where to start.

There are several simple rules I like to follow that make it easy to build a good cocktail every time. Often, things such as glass type, stirring versus shaking, and whether a cocktail has ice are about chemistry and what happens to the flavor profile when the spirit opens up in a wide glass or is bruised with citrus juice or when water is added. You can certainly have your cocktail any way you like, but skipping the ice or changing the type of glass alters the results in surprisingly significant ways.

Behold the heralding clink of ice in glass at 5:00 p.m., the happy song of a cocktail shaker with spirits chilling inside, the offering of fellowship to friends and family. The transformation from our work selves to our true selves becomes seamless through the rituals of cocktail hour."

I also believe that measuring ingredients is the only way to consistently create the perfect cocktail. A mere quarter-of-an-ounce difference can drastically alter a cocktail. Don't risk it, friends. Use a jigger. And if you don't want to be at the bar making cocktails all night, I recommend batching. All the recipes in this book batch beautifully. Simply convert the ounce measurements to a "part," which can be an ounce, a cup, a gallon, or any other measurement you choose. If the cocktail is meant to be shaken or stirred, add approximately one-quarter part water to the batch to account for the dilution that normally happens when ice is added to the shaker or mixing glass.

Shake or Stir?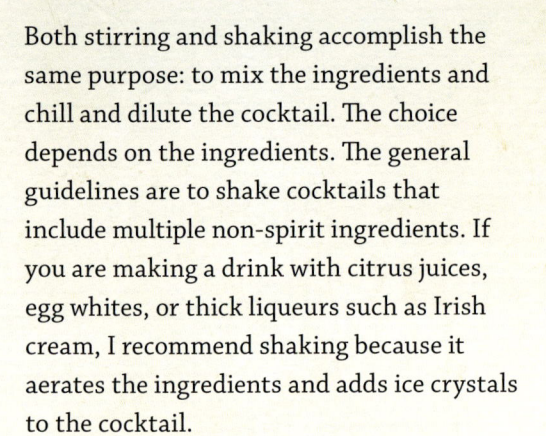

Both stirring and shaking accomplish the same purpose: to mix the ingredients and chill and dilute the cocktail. The choice depends on the ingredients. The general guidelines are to shake cocktails that include multiple non-spirit ingredients. If you are making a drink with citrus juices, egg whites, or thick liqueurs such as Irish cream, I recommend shaking because it aerates the ingredients and adds ice crystals to the cocktail.

If you are making a spirit-forward cocktail such as a Manhattan, Old-Fashioned, or Negroni, stirring is best. Stirring combines, chills, and dilutes the cocktail ingredients in a controlled manner without incorporating air or ice crystals, resulting in a perfectly clear, cold, spirit-forward drink. Some cocktails should be built in the glass, including Collins cocktails, mules, toddies, and mojitos.

Glass Type and Serving Style

In all the recipes, I include glass type and whether the cocktail is served "up" (stirred or shaken with ice and then strained into a chilled glass without ice) or "on the rocks" (with ice). A single spirit is the only drink

served "neat" (straight from the bottle to the glass, with no ice). A cocktail served up is designed to be consumed in less than 10 minutes in a few swallows before the cocktail gets warm. A cocktail served on the rocks may be nursed a bit longer, and the drink changes as the ice melts. A pour neat, straight from the bottle into a glass with no chilling or diluting, is the classic way to sip and savor a spirit for as long as you like.

"Measuring ingredients is the only way to consistently create the perfect cocktail."

One of the missions of this book is to describe the iconic classic cocktails so that when you read a cocktail menu or want to be creative at home, you will be able to recognize which family the cocktail belongs to. I believe that educated imbibers order more adventurous cocktails when they are out and collect more bottles for their own bars if they know what to do with them. Each chapter contains a note on "foundation ingredients," identifying the essence of the cocktail. Much like Julia Child's master recipes or Escoffier's mother sauces, these foundation ingredients were created decades ago and are the base for the classics and the variations that came after. For example, the basic Old-Fashioned is spirit, sugar, bitters, and water, but each of these components can vary. The spirit can be bourbon, rye, brandy, or tequila. The sugar can be any of our Make & Muddle mixers, simple syrup, an amaro, or a sweet liqueur. The bitters can be any flavor profile under the sun. The water in a cocktail is almost always about the dilution that occurs when shaking or stirring. Once you master these foundation ingredients, you can get creative.

2

INSTRUMENTS OF THE RITE

I think of rituals as acts that carry us from one headspace to another—from the "before" to the "after," no matter what the ritual is. There is meditation in movement, peace in familiarity, preparation in the performance of an act. Building a cocktail is as much about ritual as about creation for me.

There are several essential items that everyone should have on hand to build a good cocktail. Not having these bar tools won't damn you to eternal fires or prevent you from making a delicious cocktail, but it will be a little like hammering a nail with a shoe: you'll get the job done, but you may end up cursing and bleeding in the process. Bar tools are inexpensive and readily available, and full sets of bar tools can be ordered online and delivered straight to your door. That said, there have been many times when I've used a chopstick to stir my Manhattan or pulled out a measuring cup instead of a jigger, but the right tools enhance the experience and make the ritual more enjoyable. These are what I consider the necessities.

Jigger or small measure.
This is more than a shot glass. The most common jiggers have one side that is twice as large as the other side. They come in many size combinations, such as 2 oz and 1 oz, or 1 ½ oz and ¾ oz. It is also nice to have a larger 3- or 4-ounce graduated measuring glass when making multiples of the same cocktail.

Bar spoon.
This long-handled multipurpose spoon is used for stirring and measuring. The end of the handle often has a small fork used to spear garnish or a small metal ball used to break ice.

Cocktail shaker.
There are two main types of shakers: the Boston shaker, which consists of large and small tin (or glass and tin) cups, and the cobbler shaker, which consists of a tin mixing cup, a fitted strainer, and a cap for the strainer.

Muddler.
A muddler is a wood, metal, glass, or plastic cylinder used to mash cocktail ingredients in the mixing cup prior to shaking or stirring the drink. It is similar to the pestle of mortar and pestle fame. The business end of the muddler comes in many different shapes and patterns, the most basic and utilitarian being a large flat-bottomed muddler. The base can also be cut with lines or in a diamond pattern. These muddlers are good for gripping the ingredients when crushing citrus and mint for a mojito or muddling fresh fruit for a margarita.

> "Building a cocktail is as much about ritual as about creation for me."

Corkscrew or wine key. These tools come in many different shapes and styles, from the simple metal screw with a handle to the expensive automatic wine opener. Select whatever style feels most comfortable to you. In my opinion, the waiter's wine key with a hinged lever is consistent, reliable, and durable.

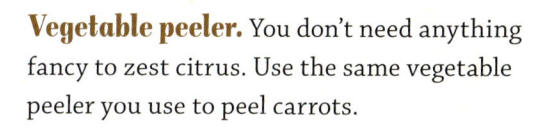

Vegetable peeler. You don't need anything fancy to zest citrus. Use the same vegetable peeler you use to peel carrots.

Cutting board and knife. To cut and trim garnishes such as citrus wedges and peels, you'll need a small paring knife and a small (6-by-8-inch) cutting board.

Mixing glass. In a pinch, just about any pint-sized glass can be used to mix one drink, but a glass with a spout and an opening large enough to accommodate a Hawthorne or julep strainer is preferable. Simple mixing glasses can be purchased for less than $20. Some well-respected bartenders use an appropriately sized beaker as a mixing glass, and I have been known to use a large mason jar. Whatever works!

Hawthorne strainer. This strainer usually consists of a metal spring and a flat metal paddle with slots to hold the spring. It fits over the top of the mixing glass or shaker containing the cocktail and the ice and strains the liquid as it is poured into the serving glass. The tighter the coil of the spring, the more material is strained out of the cocktail.

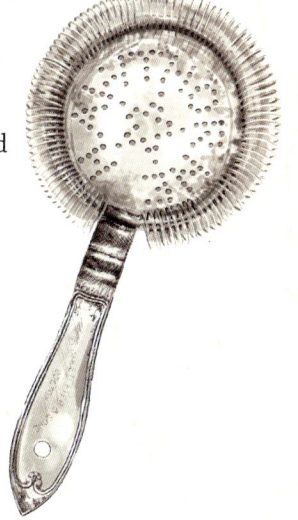

"Works of mercy abound, and you can now build a sophisticated, delicious, three-ingredient cocktail at home."

Handheld mesh strainer.
This is a smaller version of the strainer you use to drain pasta. It should be small enough to fit over a cocktail shaker. In addition to straining citrus pulp and seeds, it can be used to double-strain shaken cocktails to remove bits of herbs or ice shards.

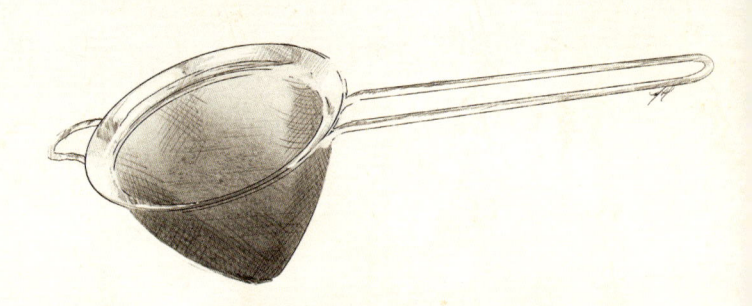

Handheld juicer. A two-part hinged metal juicer is simple, elegant, and durable. These juicers are frequently found in three different sizes and colors: green (small, for limes), yellow (medium, for lemons), and orange (large, for oranges).

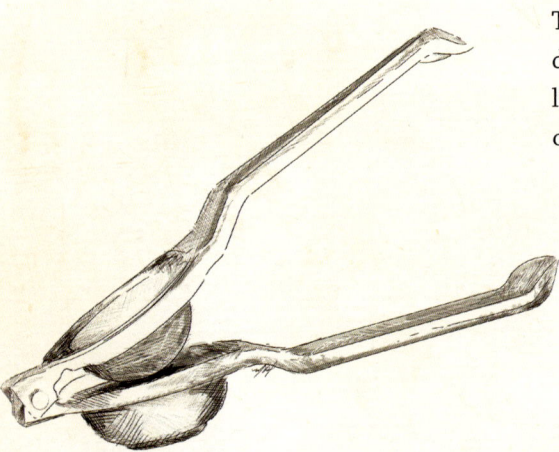

Various bottles, jars, and squeeze bottles. It's nice to have containers of several different sizes on hand. I use both new and recycled bottles such as empty liquor bottles with cork caps, jam jars, and canning jars.

Mortar and pestle. In addition to grinding or cracking spices, a mortar and pestle can be used as a muddler in a pinch.

"I do not need a single-use anything on my bar, whether spirit, ingredient, or mixer. If it cannot transition from one spirit, mood, or season to the next, I won't invest in it."

3

The Spirit

The spirit is the heart of the cocktail. It drives the flavor profile, so it should be steadfast in its quality and pure in its distillation. For everyday purposes, your bar should contain the spirits you use regularly, along with a few liqueurs and mixers. Having a well-stocked bar is just as important as having a well-stocked pantry, and with everything you need at your fingertips, it's easier to be creative. If, like me, you are a collector, you will take advantage of clearance deals on liqueurs or rare releases of items you simply must have. Collect away, friends. You are limited only by the storage space you have available. A new liqueur for your coffee or a new vermouth to try in your Manhattan is never a bad idea and can renew your creative spirit. It's certainly not an exhaustive list, but here are my recommendations for the basics.

Liquor

- Vodka
- Gin
- White and dark rum
- Blanco tequila
- Bourbon
- Rye
- Brandy

Liqueurs

- Campari or Aperol
- Vermouth—sweet and dry
- Cointreau or orange curaçao

Mixers

- Tonic water
- Club soda or seltzer water
- Ginger beer
- Juices (lemon, orange, lime, grapefruit, cranberry) and fresh citrus

- Bitters—aromatic, orange, and Peychaud's to start; grapefruit, molasses, chocolate, and tiki are also good to have on hand
- Sodas, such as cola, grapefruit, and lemon-lime

A Psalm for Bourbon

I could write a praise song to most spirits: an ode to vodka for its pure, clean flavor and flexibility in cocktails; an anthem to tequila for its simultaneous complexity and humble versatility; a hymn to rum for its depth of flavor and terroir; a canticle to gin for its crisp, herbal finish and its ability to elevate cocktails. The list could go on and on. But I am from Kentucky, so bourbon brings me to rapture. In 2015 I took my passion to the next level by becoming an executive bourbon steward. I knew what I loved about bourbon but wanted some scientific information from distillers and some sensory training. I came away with the tools I needed to welcome clients and friends to the world of bourbon whiskey, not just because I love the spirit but also because I love what bourbon represents to me.

The harried pace of our everyday lives can leave us feeling isolated and lonely at times. Bourbon appeals to what many of us want: history, tradition, legacy, and connection. It also provides a reason to slow down and savor the present moment. The good conversations that happen over a good pour are typically my favorite moments. The liquid in the glass represents years of tradition, and that whiskey does not happen in an instant. It requires expertise, resources, time, and patience.

The bourbon industry has exploded in recent years. Marketing prophets have conjured a "bourbon lifestyle" that whips the masses into a frenzy. This drives up costs and certainly sells bottles, but a lot is lost in the translation. This marketing strategy is like the difference between reading a study guide and actually reading the book. You can get a feeling about bourbon from slick marketing campaigns, on-trend bars, and hyped bottles, but the truth is in the *experience* of bourbon—in the tastings, the sensory participation, the shared experience of a good whiskey, the knowledge of how it's made, and the connection with the land and water that make Kentucky bourbon taste the way it does.

All bourbon is whiskey, but not all whiskey is bourbon. Whether your whiskey is spelled *whiskey* or *whisky* depends entirely on where you live. It is a simple formula:

Any country that has an *e* in its name spells *whiskey* with an *e* (e.g., United States, Ireland). The others do not (e.g., Canada, Scotland, Japan).

The bourbon-making process is similar to that for other distilled spirits. A mash bill (or grain recipe) is created from a combination of corn, barley, rye, and wheat. The mash is then cooked, distilled, barreled, and aged. This brief explanation greatly oversimplifies the process, which involves vast amounts of time, work, knowledge, finesse, and exceptional palates from master distillers and master tasters.

Bourbon is a federally regulated product that must adhere to a few commandments:

- It must be at least 51 percent corn.

- It must be distilled to no more than 160 proof.

- It must be aged in new, charred oak barrels.

- It must go into the barrel at no more than 125 proof.

- It can have no additional flavorings added to it.

Contrary to popular belief, there is no age limit on bourbon. If it is younger than four years old, the label on the bottle must state that, but as soon as the white dog (the

"Having a well-stocked bar is just as important as having a well-stocked pantry."

clear, unaged distilled spirit) is sealed in the new, charred oak barrel, it is considered bourbon. You wouldn't want to drink it yet, but it meets the federal criteria to be called bourbon.

Just as scotch is region-specific to Scotland, bourbon is specific to America. Although it doesn't have to be made in Kentucky to be called bourbon, Kentucky produces roughly 95 percent of the world's bourbon and, in my humble opinion, 100 percent of the world's *best* bourbon. If a label testifies that the bottle contains Kentucky Straight Bourbon Whiskey, the entire process—distilling, aging for at least two years, and bottling—must take place in Kentucky.

There are many schools of thought on why Kentucky bourbon is the best in the world. Some think it is because the oldest (and longest-producing) whiskey distilleries

in the United States are located there; some think it is because the mash bills have been perfected and handed down for generations. The land and water in Kentucky are unique, and this contributes directly to the bourbon's flavor. And as we know, a finished product is only as good as the ingredients it contains. Kentucky bourbon uses local grains and the region's limestone-filtered water—two things that set it apart from any other bourbon. In addition, the seasons and varied temperatures in Kentucky create the perfect conditions for aging in barrels.

In recent years, distilleries from New York to Oregon and everywhere in between have produced some delicious and exciting bourbon whiskeys. The unique conditions in these states—from local organic grains to snow meltwater sources—contribute directly to the flavor profiles of their bourbons. Terroir exists not only in wine but also in distilled spirits.

Although grain and water are the foundations for the best whiskeys in the world, the real magic (and science) of bourbon happens inside the barrel. The oak barrels are charred at a cooperage that builds and chars barrels specifically for the aging of spirits. The char can vary from a short char to a char that looks like alligator skin and everything in between, depending on the distillery's preference. The char also acts as a natural carbon filter to remove impurities in the bourbon. Some distilleries also toast—heating without flame—their barrels before the char. This helps release the sweet vanilla, caramel, and butterscotch notes we love in bourbon. All this heat and fire applied to the barrel is a vital part of the finished bourbon's flavor profile.

Once the whiskey is inside the barrel, the seasonal heat and cold cause the barrels to expand and contract, drawing the bourbon in and out of the wood. This time in the barrel is when all the best things happen—age, color, and flavor. Some distilleries climate-control their rickhouses—the warehouses where bourbon is stored and aged—to try to produce more consistent results. But no matter what anyone says, time is time inside a barrel. You can't cheat when it comes to the aging process.

Some distilleries include age statements on their labels, but this is not required unless the bourbon is less than four years old. The age statement must reflect the youngest bourbon used in any bottle. For example, if a distillery is blending barrels of ten-, eight-, and six-year-old bourbon for its current release, the age stated on the label must be six years old.

"The spirit is the heart of the cocktail."

The Tasting Process

There is a basic four-part process for tasting bourbon. A good glass enhances the experience. I recommend a Glencairn whiskey-tasting glass with a base that is wider than the opening. They can be found online or at many retailers.

Sensory training is a skill that improves with practice. You can find tasting notes on distilleries' websites or in any number of bourbon blogs. But try to identify the flavors without a prompt and then check the tasting notes after your first taste. The more you do it, the better you'll become.

After the pour, assess these four elements:

Appearance. What color is it? How dark is it compared to other bourbons? This depends on age and barrel "recipe" (toast and char).

Aroma or nose. What smells do you recognize? Maple? Caramel? Vanilla? Smoke? Like wine tasting, whiskey tasting has its own descriptive vocabulary.

Taste. The first mouthful of bourbon should coat the inside of your mouth. Many in the business call this the "Kentucky chew," which prepares the palate to taste

> **"Sensory training is a skill that improves with practice."**

the nuances of the whiskey. Your eyes tear up, your mouth waters, and your tongue burns with the first sip. With the second sip, the real tasting begins. What do you taste? Burnt sugar? Citrus? Spices?

Finish. The finish is what lingers after you swallow. If the taste stays for a while, the bourbon has a long finish. If the taste dissipates quickly, it has a short finish. What do you taste after you swallow? Butterscotch? Honey? Cream? Tobacco? Spice? Heat?

The most important thing to remember when tasting bourbon or any other spirit is that there are no right or wrong answers. Everyone has a different palate, and you taste what you taste. Tasting notes are a great guide, but we all bring different experiences to each sip. As you taste many different bourbons and expand your experiences, you are training your senses to pick out subtle flavors.

This tasting process can be utilized with any spirit, whether whiskey, tequila, rum, gin, or anything else. It helps you decide why you like what you like. Knowing that you like bourbon with tobacco notes or tequila with vegetal notes can guide your future purchases. Education is empowering. Through sensory training and practice, you'll become better at pulling apart flavor profiles. It's thirsty work, but the payoff is grand. I recommend lots and lots of practice, preferably with friends.

4

Infused Simple Syrups

We have all sinned and fallen short in the creation of a perfect cocktail. My brothers and sisters, I am here to shepherd you to that heavenly place where there is no suffering, only beautiful, delicious cocktails. That journey can take many paths, but know that you will not walk alone. I will be with you no matter which one you choose.

One of the first steps to bring your cocktail closer to heaven is making your own simple syrup. This versatile, accurately named ingredient can be made with inexpensive items found in almost every kitchen. And if you run out, the ingredients for simple syrup can be found at any gas station convenience store for those times when emergency cocktails are required. Even if you are in the desert with no supplies in sight, it is better to use what you have on hand rather than settle for a vexing cocktail.

"We have all sinned and fallen short in the creation of a perfect cocktail."

Simple syrup is one of the most basic ingredients in cocktails. It is also great for sweetening other chilled beverages such as iced tea and iced coffee. At Make & Muddle, we have done the work for you: you can use our mixers to enjoy a beautiful, sophisticated craft cocktail. Or, if you want to make your own simple syrup, the basic recipe is 1 part sugar plus 1 part water. Add the sugar and water to a pan on the stove, stir, and bring it to a boil. Once the sugar is dissolved, remove it from the heat, cool the syrup, and store it in the refrigerator for up to a month.

When I was brought low by plain simple syrup in a cocktail, infused syrups saved me. Using the 1:1 formula as a foundation, you can steep virtually anything in the hot syrup to change the flavor—herbs, spices, fruits, or any combination. Citrus zest is one of my favorites and can brighten any cocktail.

Steeping times vary from ingredient to ingredient and also depend on your taste preference. To steep, remove the finished syrup from the heat, add flavor agents, stir, and cover for the desired length of time. For example, my mint julep recipe calls for mint syrup. I steep the mint for 24 hours because I want a concentrated mint flavor for that cocktail. I find this is true of citrus syrups as well. You really can't steep them too long. Other ingredients such as lavender and cinnamon require less time because their flavors can quickly overpower a cocktail.

Sugar Types

Sugars add another layer of flavor to syrups, and there are many types to choose from. I prefer organic cane sugar, not only because it is organic but also because of the viscosity it gives the syrup and therefore the cocktail as well.

Refined white sugar. The five-pound bag of sugar at the grocery store is made of either natural cane or beets and produces a straightforward sweet, colorless, clear simple syrup. This is a good sugar to use when you don't want the syrup to affect the color of the beverage.

Natural cane sugar. Sugar made from 100 percent sugarcane, it has a slight blonde color, distinguishing it from refined white sugar. It therefore produces a syrup that is more blonde than clear. Cane sugar has a mild sugarcane flavor—almost like someone added a drop of molasses to refined sugar. It gives cocktails a nice structure without overwhelming the flavors.

Turbinado sugar. Turbinado sugar is made from pure cane sugar extract. Its name refers to the technique used to make this sugar, which involves spinning it in a cylinder or turbine. Turbinado sugar undergoes less processing than white sugar and retains a slight molasses flavor. It produces a slightly darker syrup than natural cane sugar. Sugar in the Raw is one brand of turbinado sugar.

Demerara sugar. Demerara is a light brown cane sugar originally from Guyana. It produces a syrup similar in color to light brown sugar.

Light and dark brown sugars.

Traditionally, brown sugar is what's left after refined white sugar has gone through the evaporator. Modern brown sugar is most likely refined white sugar with molasses added—less molasses for light brown sugar (typically 3.5 percent) and more for dark brown sugar (typically 6.5 percent), according to baking expert Rose Levy Beranbaum. They perform virtually the same way, although dark brown sugar has a deeper molasses flavor profile. Brown sugars produce darker syrups that work well with darker spirits.

Muscovado sugar.

This amazingly rich sugar from Africa is unrefined cane sugar containing molasses—labeled either "light" (with less molasses) or "dark" (with more molasses). It is not as dry as other sugars and has an intense molasses flavor. It produces a dark, rich syrup.

Piloncillo or panela.

Commonly found in Latin groceries, this sugar is made of cane juice that has been boiled down to a thick, crystalline syrup and then poured into cone-shaped molds to harden. The rich flavor profile makes it ideal for achieving depth of flavor. It produces a syrup similar in color to one made with dark brown sugar but not as dark as one made with muscovado sugar. This is one of the sugars used in Make & Muddle's 7 Syrup to give it an amazing deep molasses color and flavor.

Traditional Simple Syrup

1 cup sugar
1 cup water

Brown Sugar/Demerara Simple Syrup (SS)

1 cup packed light or dark brown sugar
1 cup water

Mint Syrup

1 recipe traditional simple syrup
1 large handful mint leaves and stems

Steep for at least 6 hours and as long as 24 hours. Strain through a fine mesh sieve.

Cinnamon Syrup

1 recipe traditional simple syrup
4 sticks cinnamon

Steep for at least an hour. Strain through a fine mesh sieve.

Vanilla Simple Syrup

1 recipe traditional simple syrup
1 whole vanilla bean, split lengthwise

Scrape the vanilla seeds into the syrup, add the pod, and steep for at least an hour. Strain through a fine mesh sieve.

Lavender Syrup

1 recipe traditional simple syrup
3 tbsp. culinary lavender

Steep the lavender—either loose or in a tea ball—for less than an hour, as lavender can quickly overpower other flavors. Strain through a fine mesh sieve.

Lemon or Lime Syrup

1 recipe traditional simple syrup
Peel from 2 lemons or 2 limes

Steep for at least 3 hours. Strain through a fine mesh sieve.

Jalapeño Syrup

1 recipe traditional simple syrup
2–3 whole jalapeños, including seeds, chopped

Steep for at least 3 hours. Strain through a fine mesh sieve.

Herb Syrup

1 recipe traditional simple syrup
5–7 stems fresh thyme
4 stems fresh rosemary
2–3 stems fresh sage

Steep for at least 3 hours. Strain through a fine mesh sieve.

Basil Syrup

1 recipe traditional simple syrup
1 large handful fresh basil, including stems

Cover and steep for as long as possible, up to 24 hours. Strain through a fine mesh sieve.

Cinnamon Orange Syrup

1 recipe traditional simple syrup
Peel from 1 navel orange
4 sticks cinnamon

Steep for at least an hour. Strain through a fine mesh sieve.

If you prefer to avoid cooking, Make & Muddle has done the work for you, so you can just pour wonderful flavors out of a bottle. Here are the current offerings from Make & Muddle, followed by a do-it-yourself substitution if you want to create your own infused syrups based on the Make & Muddle flavor profiles.

7 Syrup

This flagship syrup was originally intended to be a pumpkin spice liqueur. I was looking for something seasonal, festive, and comforting that incorporated all the baking spices of fall. The recipe went through several iterations before I finally decided to omit any kind of spirit from the formula and make a syrup with deep, intense flavors. This was achieved by steeping the spices for two days prior to bottling. Although it was made with the fall and winter in mind, with seven spices and three different sugars, it also works beautifully in tropical cocktails and can even replace the aromatic bitters

in an Old-Fashioned year-round. Since 7 Syrup's inception, Make & Muddle has adopted this philosophy for all its products: keep the flavors intense and rich to produce a balanced beverage and not a watered-down sugar bomb.

7 Syrup Substitution

Makes 1 oz.

½ oz. cinnamon, clove, and nutmeg syrup
½ oz. Allspice Dram (a liqueur)

To make the spiced syrup, bring 1 cup sugar and 1 cup water to a boil. Stir until the sugar is dissolved. Remove from the heat and add 2 cinnamon sticks, 1 tsp. whole cloves, and 1 whole nutmeg cracked with a mortar and pestle. Steep for 2 hours. Strain and add the Allspice Dram. It will keep in the refrigerator for up to a month.

2 Pepper Agave Syrup

2 Pepper Agave was Make & Muddle's next mixer, and it was designed to make the best agave beverages you ever tasted. It was first released in the winter, so we used fresh citrus and 100 percent blue agave tequila to make the out-of-the-dark and into-the-light cocktail everyone craves when it's cold outside. It is also our alternative sweetener mixer, made with 100 percent organic agave, fresh serrano peppers, black pepper, coriander, and bitter orange peel. The aroma from the fresh serranos is the first thing that hits you when you open the bottle, and the sweet heat is the perfect balance of spice and flavor in any cocktail or spirit-free beverage.

2 Pepper Agave Syrup Substitution

Makes 1 oz.

½ oz. jalapeño syrup
¼ oz. simple syrup
¼ oz. orange liqueur

To make the jalapeño and simple syrups, bring 1 cup sugar and 1 cup water to a boil and stir until the sugar is dissolved. Remove from the heat and set aside ½ cup of syrup. To the remaining hot syrup, add 1 chopped jalapeño, with or without seeds (include the seeds if you like it spicy). Steep for 2 hours. Strain, combine with the simple syrup, and add the orange liqueur. It will keep in the refrigerator for up to a month.

"When I was brought low by plain simple syrup in a cocktail, infused syrups saved me."

Honey Lavender Elixir

Honey Lavender Elixir was originally designed as a toddy syrup to battle the countless colds and sore throats that plague us all during the winter months. I quickly discovered its versatility: it loves clear and brown spirits alike and is a great addition to a hot gin toddy, an ice cold Lavender 75 with gin and bubbles, or a hard lavender lemonade with vodka. Children and those who don't imbibe will love it in a spirit-free lavender lemonade or as a sweetener for iced tea.

Honey Lavender Elixir Substitution

Makes 1 oz.

½ oz. honey syrup
½ oz. lavender syrup

To make the honey syrup, measure equal parts honey and water. Heat only the water until it boils. Remove the water from the heat and add the honey, stirring until it dissolves. (Do not cook the honey and water together, as heating honey directly causes it to lose its antimicrobial and antioxidant qualities.) Store the cooled syrup in the refrigerator for up to a month.

To make the lavender syrup, bring 1 cup sugar and 1 cup water to a boil. Remove from the heat and add 3 tbsp. culinary lavender. Steep for up to 2 hours. Strain and store in the refrigerator for up to a month.

Spiced Cherry Vanilla Syrup

This syrup originated from my deep love of all things cherry. One year we had a particularly good summer for delicious Bing cherries, and I was using them to make everything I could imagine. I wanted the cherries to shine in this mixer, but I also wanted to ground it with spices so that you are drawn to the depth of flavor. Made with cherry juice from local growers in Michigan, organic cane sugar, cardamom, cinnamon, and pure vanilla extract, this syrup makes the best Manhattan you've ever had.

Make & Muddle syrups also perform exceptionally well in the kitchen. I have used this particular syrup in everything from cherry cobbler to Black Forest cake to cherry gastrique for pan-seared duck breasts. It is perfect every time and elevates traditional recipes to something truly special.

Spiced Cherry Vanilla Syrup Substitution

Makes 1¼ oz.

¼ oz. vanilla syrup
¼ oz. cinnamon syrup
½ oz. cherry juice
¼ oz. Cardamaro (an Italian liqueur)

To make the vanilla and cinnamon syrups, bring 1 cup sugar and 1 cup water to a boil. Remove from the heat and transfer half the syrup to another pan. To the first pan, add 1 whole vanilla bean, split, and seeds scraped into the pan. To the other pan, add 4 sticks cinnamon. Cover both pans and steep for 3 hours. Strain and add the cherry juice and Cardamaro. It will keep in the refrigerator for up to a month.

3 Herb Gracious Grapefruit Syrup

This syrup was designed for a mid-pandemic Thanksgiving celebration. Some friends were hosting a small group of people for the holiday and wanted to serve a signature cocktail. I wanted a cocktail that could cut through the rich gravy and carb-heavy food but also complement the herbal flavors holiday dinners are famous for. Thyme, rosemary, and sage were obvious choices. Once we had selected grapefruit and lime as the citrus base, we decided a char on the citrus would give us a nice smoke flavor. This syrup loves every spirit we ever tried it with and can easily do a bourbon Collins, a gin gimlet, a tequila Paloma, and a smoked tequila Old-Fashioned.

3 Herb Gracious Grapefruit Syrup Substitution

Makes 1 oz.

½ oz. grapefruit lime syrup
½ oz. thyme, rosemary, and sage syrup

To make the syrups, bring 1 cup sugar and 1 cup water to a boil. Remove from the heat and transfer half the syrup to another pan. To the first pan, add the peel of half a grapefruit and the peel of 1 lime. Cover and steep for at least 2 hours.

To the second pan, add 5 stems fresh thyme, 2 stems fresh rosemary, and 2 stems fresh sage and steep for up to 2 hours. Strain both syrups and store in the refrigerator for up to a month.

Orange Ginger Cranberry Shrub

This bright red shrub—Make & Muddle's first true holiday mixer—is bursting with flavor. It uses fresh cranberries from Wisconsin growers, organic sugar, brown sugar, fresh orange peel, and fresh ginger. It mixes with both brown and clear spirits and particularly likes bubbles of any kind. It looks festive in the glass and makes beautiful and delicious cocktails. Because cranberry season is so short, this mixer is available only from October through December.

Orange Ginger Cranberry Shrub Substitution

Makes 1 oz.

¼ oz. cinnamon orange syrup
¼ oz. ginger syrup (or Domaine de Canton liqueur)
½ oz. cranberry juice

To make the syrups, bring 1 cup sugar and 1 cup water to a boil. Remove from the heat and transfer half the syrup to another pan. To the first pan, add 2 sticks cinnamon and the peel of 1 orange. To the second pan, add 3 inches fresh ginger root cut into ¼-inch coins. Don't peel the ginger, as most of the flavor is in the skin; just wash it well before adding it to the syrup. Steep both syrups for at least 2 hours. Strain and add the cranberry juice. It will keep in the refrigerator for up to a month.

5

THE OLD-FASHIONED

Foundation ingredients: spirit, sugar, water, bitters

In the beginning there was spirit, and the spirit was without form. Then to this spirit, water, bitters, and sugar were added. And the cocktail was thereby created. We drank the cocktail and it was good.

The Old-Fashioned is thought to be the original cocktail. The oldest writings describe it as distilled spirit, water, sugar, and bitters. It is rumored that this cocktail earned its name after other cocktails were created and people began ordering their cocktails "the old-fashioned way," which was eventually shortened to "old-fashioned."

It is also rumored that the cocktail originated at the Pendennis Club in Louisville, Kentucky—the hometown of Make & Muddle—in 1881. Other sources mention it prior to 1881 and as early as 1690 in England. Like all stories that involve alcohol, this one's origins are a little foggy. Whether the Old-Fashioned was created in a Louisville bar or by an apothecary in England, who are we to let some silly facts get in the way of a good story?

But please, for all that is holy, avoid committing what amounts to a cardinal sin in Kentucky: don't muddle a cherry and orange and add seltzer to this drink. Luckily, Make & Muddle has created the perfect syrup for an Old-Fashioned: the 7 Syrup Cocktail Mixer. Old-Fashioneds do not have to be made exclusively with brown spirits. Also included are a few nontraditional recipes that are just as good as the original bourbon cocktail.

The Old-Fashioned

Glass: Old-Fashioned
Served: On the rocks
Yield: 1 drink

2 oz. bourbon
1 tsp. sugar
1 tsp. water
Dash bitters
Orange peel for garnish

Add the sugar, water, and bitters to a mixing glass. Stir until the sugar is dissolved. Add bourbon and ice and stir until very cold. Strain into an Old-Fashioned glass with fresh ice and garnish with orange peel.

Make & Muddle Old-Fashioned

Glass: Old-Fashioned
Served: On the rocks
Yield: 1 drink

2 oz. Kentucky straight bourbon
½ oz. Make & Muddle 7 Syrup (or substitute; see chapter 4)
Dash orange bitters
Dash aromatic bitters
Orange peel and Amarena cherry for garnish

In a mixing glass with ice, add the bourbon, syrup, and bitters and stir until cold. Strain from the mixing glass into an Old-Fashioned glass with ice. Garnish with a cherry and orange peel, expressing the oils over the drink and around the rim of the glass.

"In the beginning there was spirit, and the spirit was without form."

Auld-Farrant

Glass: Old-Fashioned
Served: On the rocks
Yield: 1 drink

2 oz. single-malt scotch
½ oz. Make & Muddle Honey Lavender Elixir (or substitute; see chapter 4)
Dash orange or lemon bitters
Lemon peel for garnish

In a mixing glass with ice, add the scotch, Honey Lavender Elixir, and bitters and stir until cold. Strain from the mixing glass into an Old-Fashioned glass with ice. Garnish with lemon peel, expressing the oils over the drink and around the rim of the glass.

Barrel-Aged Gin Old-Fashioned

Glass: Old-Fashioned
Served: On the rocks
Yield: 1 drink

2 oz. barrel-aged gin
½ oz. Make & Muddle Honey Lavender Elixir (or substitute; see chapter 4)
Dash lemon bitters
Lemon peel for garnish

In a mixing glass with ice, add the gin, Honey Lavender Elixir, and bitters and stir until cold. Strain from the mixing glass into an Old-Fashioned glass with ice. Garnish with lemon peel, expressing the oils over the drink and around the rim of the glass.

Spiced Cherry Old-Fashioned

Glass: Old-Fashioned
Served: On the rocks
Yield: 1 drink

2 oz. dark rum (preferably single barrel)
½ oz. Make & Muddle Spiced Cherry Vanilla
Syrup (or substitute; see chapter 4)
Dash molasses or chocolate bitters
Lemon peel and Amarena cherry for garnish

In a mixing glass with ice, add the rum,
syrup, and bitters and stir until cold. Strain
from the mixing glass into an Old-Fashioned
glass with ice. Garnish with a cherry and
lemon peel, expressing the oils over the
drink and around the rim of the glass.

Most regions of the world have their own
spirits: scotch from Scotland, sake from
Japan, tequila from Mexico, bourbon
from the United States, wine from Italy,
champagne from France, raki from Turkey,
and aquavit from Scandinavia. Aquavit is
made from distilling grains or potatoes and
then adding savory flavors such as fennel,
caraway (rye), and dill. It can be bottled
directly or aged. Some say that aquavit is an
acquired taste. The first time I tried it was
with a good friend of mine from Sweden, who
compared the taste to high school regret.
From my perspective, though, it provides
exactly what I like in a spirit: It's high proof
and herbal forward, and it has the potential
to work in both sweet and savory cocktails.
It's tasty enough to be the star of a spirit-
forward cocktail and flexible enough to add
depth to a cocktail with other ingredients. It
also makes a killer Bloody Mary.

The pairing of aquavit and 3 Herb Gracious
Grapefruit syrup in this Old-Fashioned is a
good fit. The citrus plays well with the spirit,
and the herbs from the aquavit and the syrup
are a party in your mouth. Skål!

Copenhagen After Dark

Glass: Old-Fashioned
Served: On the rocks
Yield: 1 drink

2 oz. barrel-aged aquavit
½ oz. Make & Muddle 3 Herb Gracious
Grapefruit syrup (or substitute; see chapter
4)
Dash grapefruit bitters
Dash Copper & Kings alembic bitters
Grapefruit or lemon peel for garnish

In a mixing glass with ice, add the aquavit,
syrup, and bitters and stir until cold. Strain
from the mixing glass into an Old-Fashioned
glass with ice. Garnish with grapefruit or
lemon peel, expressing the oils over the
drink and around the rim of the glass.

Smoked Cocktails

Smoking is a great way to infuse flavor into a cocktail. Smoking kits are available online, but here are the basics you'll need:

- Solid wood coaster or cutting board
- Smoking chips or dried herbs of your choice
- Lighter
- Coaster
- Old-Fashioned glass
- Ice water

Before you start, fill the glass with ice water. Prepare the smoking chips or dried herbs on the wooden coaster or cutting board and light them to start them burning. Dump the water out of the glass and place the open end over the smoking chips, allowing it to capture the smoke. Once the glass is filled with smoke, quickly turn it over and cover the rim with a coaster to trap the smoke inside. Meanwhile, build the cocktail in a mixing glass. Lift the coaster, add ice to the

51

smoke-filled glass, and quickly replace it to prevent the smoke from escaping. When the cocktail is ready, remove the coaster and strain the cocktail into the glass.

I love the Make & Muddle Old-Fashioned, but the smoked tequila Old-Fashioned is delicious. The smoke from the tequila and the char from the citrus in the 3 Herb Gracious Grapefruit Syrup are perfect together.

Smoked Tequila Old-Fashioned

Glass: Old-Fashioned
Served: On the rocks
Yield: 1 drink

2 oz. reposado tequila
½ oz. Make & Muddle 3 Herb Gracious
Grapefruit Syrup (or substitute; see chapter 4)
Dash lime, lemon, or grapefruit bitters
Dried sage leaves for smoking
Fresh or dried sage leaves or grapefruit peel
for garnish

Follow the preceding directions for building
a smoked cocktail. Garnish with fresh or
dried sage leaves or grapefruit peel and
enjoy!

Fat Washing

Nothing says top shelf like a fat-washed cocktail. This process may seem intimidating at first, and although it does have a few steps, it is really quite simple. And it can create a wonderful ingredient for cocktails and culinary endeavors alike.

Fat washing is the process by which fat is added to a spirit and then strained out. The rationale is twofold: to infuse flavor into the spirit and to remove other undesirable flavors and characteristics from the spirit. The quick scientific explanation is that the added fats bond with the polyphenols in the spirit. Polyphenols are naturally occurring chemicals that can cause astringent flavors. When the fat is removed from the spirit, the polyphenols are removed as well. This can smooth the edges of a spirit, whether it is a higher-proof or a lower-quality spirit.

Infusion is a two-way street. You create not only a flavor-infused spirit but also a spirit-

"Fat washing is the process by which fat is added to a spirit and then strained out."

infused fat. This fat can be used in many ways, from baking with rum-infused butter to using bourbon-infused bacon fat to sauté onions.

The basics of fat washing are the same regardless of the spirit you use. To make fat-washed whiskey, you will need two 1-quart mason jars or swing-arm jars; a fine mesh cone strainer; a wooden spoon; 1 cup 100-proof, bottled-in-bond bourbon; and ½ cup rendered bacon fat, warm enough to pour through the strainer but not so hot that it splatters when it hits the alcohol. Pour the bourbon into a jar. Place the strainer over the mouth of the jar and pour the bacon fat through the strainer to catch any solid pieces. Close the jar and give it a good shake.

Leave it on the counter for a couple of hours, shaking it every 15 minutes or so. Then place the jar in the refrigerator until the bacon fat is hard. With the handle of a wooden spoon, break up the bacon fat. Pour the liquid through the strainer into a clean jar. Save the bacon fat caught in the strainer to use in the kitchen for anything from caramelizing onions to searing steaks. Put the fat-infused bourbon in a bottle and label it with the date it was fat-washed. Fat-washed spirits should be stored in the refrigerator or freezer and used within a week or two. A good rule of thumb for storage time is how long you would store the product used to infuse the spirit

Fat-Washed Old-Fashioned

Glass: Old-Fashioned
Served: On the rocks
Yield: 1 drink

2 oz. fat-washed bourbon
½ oz. Make & Muddle 7 Syrup (or substitute; see chapter 4)
Dash orange bitters
Orange peel and Amarena cherries for garnish

In a mixing glass with ice, add the bourbon, syrup, and bitters and stir until cold. Strain from the mixing glass into an Old-Fashioned glass with ice. Garnish with orange peel and cherries.

Infusing with brown butter is another way to fat-wash spirits. Brown butter is butter that has been heated until most of the moisture has evaporated and the remaining milk solids are toasted. This process gives the butter a delicious nutty flavor. Brown butter and rum go together like peas and carrots.

To make brown butter, melt a stick of butter over medium heat, stirring occasionally to ensure even melting. Once the butter begins to steam and foam, start stirring. This requires your full attention, as the butter can burn in the blink of an eye. When the milk solids turn a toasty brown color, remove the pan from the heat and pour the butter into a container, scraping all the bits from the pan. Let it cool for a few minutes.

Meanwhile, add 1 cup dark rum to a 1-quart mason jar or swing-arm jar. When the butter has cooled enough not to splatter, pour it into the jar. Straining is not necessary, as you want all the bits of toasted butter in the rum. Close the jar and shake. Leave it on the counter for at least 2 hours, shaking it every 15 minutes or so. Then place the jar in the refrigerator until the butter has solidified. With the handle of a wooden spoon, break up the butter. Pour the liquid through a fine mesh cone strainer into a clean jar. Save the butter caught in the strainer to use in the kitchen for anything from baked goods to butter on your pancakes. Put the butter-infused rum in a bottle and label it with the date it was fat-washed. Fat-washed spirits should be stored in the refrigerator or freezer and used within a week or two.

A third method of fat washing is also the quickest: add the fat directly to the cocktail when mixing it. For example, you could add olive oil to a martini or sesame oil to a Manhattan. Just add the oil to the shaker, shake, and double-strain the cocktail through a Hawthorne strainer and then a fine mesh strainer into the glass.

Brown Butter Rum Old-Fashioned

Glass: Old-Fashioned
Served: On the rocks
Yield: 1 drink

2 oz. brown butter rum
½ oz. demerara syrup
Dash aromatic bitters
Orange peel for garnish

In a mixing glass with ice, add the rum, syrup, and bitters and stir until cold. Strain from the mixing glass into an Old-Fashioned glass with ice. Garnish with orange peel.

"Infusion is a two-way street. You create not only a flavor-infused spirit but also a spirit-infused fat."

6

The Manhattan

Foundation ingredients: spirit, vermouth, bitters, water

The Manhattan doesn't get as much attention as the Old-Fashioned, so I am here to make Manhattan disciples of my fellow cocktail evangelists. This is my go-to cocktail, my alpha and omega, my beginning- and end-of-the-evening favorite. The pairing of spirit and sweet vermouth is a combination I didn't know I needed until this cocktail was sent down from the heavens.

Cocktail history is difficult to pin down, and as a result, we have several versions of the "true origin" of the Manhattan. The earliest written mention was apparently in 1882 when the *Sunday Morning Herald* of Olean, New York, noted, "It is but a short time ago that a mixture of whiskey, vermouth, and bitters came into vogue." The recipe shows up in 1884 in the iconic cocktail cookbook *The Modern Bartender's Guide* by O. H. Byron.

Another story claims that the Manhattan was created in 1874 by Lady Randolph Churchill (Winston Churchill's mother) at a banquet she was throwing to celebrate the successful gubernatorial campaign of Samuel Jones Tilden. Famed cocktail historian David Wondrich has disproved this account, as the lady in question was in England giving birth to Winston when this particular banquet took place.

"I am here to make Manhattan disciples of my fellow cocktail evangelists."

A traditional Manhattan recipe consists of whiskey, vermouth, and bitters. If we assume this cocktail was founded in New York, the original recipe probably called for rye whiskey, since New York is primarily rye country. Bourbon is commonly used as well, especially in Kentucky. I think equal parts bourbon and rye make the best Manhattan.

There are three types of Manhattans: a dry Manhattan, made with dry or French vermouth; a perfect Manhattan, made with equal parts sweet and dry vermouth; and a sweet Manhattan, made with sweet or Italian vermouth. Vermouth is a fortified wine, meaning that a distilled spirit is added to raise the alcohol by volume (ABV); it often has other flavorings too, such as herbs or bittering ingredients. Although sweet vermouth is traditionally referred to as Italian vermouth and dry vermouth as French vermouth, vermouth is not region specific and can be made anywhere in the world. There are many delicious brands on the market, and I encourage you to try as many as you can. It is also worth noting that you should treat vermouth like any other bottle of wine and refrigerate it after opening.

The Manhattan is traditionally served straight up in a coupe glass. It can also be served on the rocks or with one big rock in a rocks or Old-Fashioned glass. However you want to experience the cocktail is perfectly acceptable.

The Manhattan

Glass: Coupe or rocks
Served: Up or on the rocks
Yield: 1 drink

2 oz. rye whiskey
1 oz. sweet vermouth
Dash aromatic bitters
Amarena cherry for garnish

Add the ingredients to a mixing glass with ice. Stir until very cold. Strain into a chilled coupe glass without ice or a rocks glass with one large ice cube. Garnish with a cherry.

Make & Muddle Manhattan

Glass: Coupe or rocks
Served: Up or on the rocks
Yield: 1 drink

1 oz. bourbon
1 oz. rye
¾ oz. Make & Muddle Spiced Cherry Vanilla
Syrup (or substitute; see chapter 4)
¼ oz. Antica vermouth
Dash orange bitters
Amarena cherry for garnish

Add the ingredients to a mixing glass with
ice. Stir until very cold. Strain into a chilled
coupe glass without ice or a rocks glass with
one large ice cube. Garnish with a cherry.

Brandy Manhattan

Glass: Coupe or rocks
Served: Up or on the rocks
Yield: 1 drink

2 oz. brandy
¾ oz. Make & Muddle Spiced Cherry Vanilla
Syrup (or substitute; see chapter 4)
¼ oz. Antica vermouth
Dash aromatic bitters
Amarena cherry for garnish

Add the ingredients to a mixing glass with
ice. Stir until very cold. Strain into a chilled
coupe glass without ice or a rocks glass with
one large ice cube. Garnish with a cherry.

Tequila Manhattan

Glass: Coupe or rocks
Served: Up or on the rocks
Yield: 1 drink

2 oz. tequila
½ oz. dry vermouth
½ oz. Make & Muddle 3 Herb Gracious
Grapefruit Syrup (or substitute; see chapter 4)
Dash grapefruit bitters
Grapefruit or lime peel for garnish

Add the ingredients to a mixing glass with
ice. Stir until very cold. Strain into a chilled
coupe glass without ice or a rocks glass with
one large ice cube. Garnish with grapefruit
or lime peel.

Dry Manhattan

Glass: Coupe or rocks
Served: Up or on the rocks
Yield: 1 drink

2 oz. bourbon
½ oz. Make & Muddle Honey Lavender
Elixir (or substitute; see chapter 4)
½ oz. dry vermouth
Dash orange bitters
Grapefruit or lime peel for garnish

Add the ingredients to a mixing glass with
ice. Stir until very cold. Strain into a chilled
coupe glass without ice or a rocks glass with
one large ice cube. Garnish with grapefruit
or lime peel.

Devil's Bluegrass

Glass: Coupe or rocks
Served: Up or on the rocks
Yield: 1 drink

2 oz. bourbon
½ oz. Antica vermouth
½ oz. Make & Muddle 7 Syrup (or substitute; see chapter 4)
Dash Peychaud's bitters
Grapefruit or lime peel for garnish

Add the ingredients to a mixing glass with ice. Stir until very cold. Strain into a chilled coupe glass without ice or a rocks glass with one large ice cube. Garnish with grapefruit or lime peel.

Perfect Havana

Glass: Coupe or rocks
Served: Up or on the rocks
Yield: 1 drink

2 oz. dark rum, preferably single barrel
½ oz. Antica vermouth
½ oz. Contratto vermouth
Dash molasses bitters
Orange peel for garnish

Add the ingredients to a mixing glass with ice. Stir until very cold. Strain into a chilled coupe glass without ice or a rocks glass with one large ice cube. Garnish with orange peel.

Maverick

Glass: Coupe or rocks
Served: Up or on the rocks
Yield: 1 drink

2 oz. bourbon
1 oz. yellow Chartreuse
½ oz. Antica vermouth
½ oz. Make & Muddle Honey Lavender Elixir (or substitute; see chapter 4)
Dash aromatic bitters
Orange peel for garnish

Add the ingredients to a mixing glass with ice. Stir until very cold. Strain into a chilled coupe glass without ice or a rocks glass with one large ice cube. Garnish with orange peel.

> "The pairing of spirit and sweet vermouth is a combination I didn't know I needed until this cocktail was sent down from the heavens."

7

Sours

Foundation ingredients: spirit, sugar, citrus, water

I have plans for you, my fellow cocktail evangelists—plans for delicious cocktails that are blessedly batchable and will restore your hope and faith in cocktails made by the pitcher (see chapter 1 for batching guidelines). The sour family is one of the oldest categories of cocktails. The sour can trace its roots to the early maritime practice of including alcohol in sailors' rations and adding lemon or lime to prevent scurvy, sugar to enhance palatability, and water to prevent excess drunkenness. The earliest mention of the sour in writing is a handwritten list of 107 cocktails offered at Mart Ackerman's Saloon in Toronto, Canada, in 1856. Next, the sour is mentioned in the famed 1862 cocktail cookbook *The Bartender's Guide*.

Many cocktails spring from this well. The whiskey sour is the most common, followed by the margarita ("daisy" in Spanish), which is considered a sour because it contains spirit (tequila), citrus, sweetener, water (from ice dilution), and sometimes curaçao. Bourbon is my path to rapture, but tequila can also deliver me. Tequila is specific to Mexico. According to the Norma Oficial Mexicana (NOM) for tequila—the regulations governing its production—51 percent of the sugar used to make tequila must come from the blue Weber agave plant, which must be grown on a registered plantation in one of 180 municipalities located in five states: Jalisco, Nayarit, Guanajuato, Michoacán, and Tamaulipas. The agave must be processed,

fermented, distilled, and aged by an authorized producer in one of these 180 municipalities. Bottling is the only activity that can occur outside these approved areas. Tequila doesn't have to be 100 percent blue agave, but that's what I recommend.

There are three different types of tequila. Blanco (silver) tequila has only water added to dilute it to the desired proof before being bottled. It is, as one distillery owner told me, "Mexico without makeup." It has the purest flavor and offers the best opportunity to taste all the notes in the tequila. Reposado ("rested") tequila has been aged in oak barrels for at least two months. It is a mellower version of blanco. The barrel rounds some of the spirit's edges and gives it a little color and the lovely flavor notes added by oak. Like the vanilla and caramel of a good bourbon or the smoke and tobacco of a good rye, the barrel teases those flavors out of the spirit. Añejo ("old") tequila has been aged in oak barrels for one to three years. It is marvelous for sipping over a big rock, the same way you would enjoy a good whiskey. The extended barrel time matures the tequila and smooths all its raw edges, creating something more refined.

The Margarita

Glass: Rocks
Served: On the rocks
Yield: 1 drink

2 oz. blanco tequila
2 oz. lime juice
1 oz. orange curaçao
1 oz. simple syrup
Lime wedges for glass prep and garnish

Prepare the glass by running a lime wedge around the rim and then dipping the rim into a mixture of 1 cup sugar and 1 tbsp. kosher salt. Add the ingredients to a cocktail shaker with ice. Shake until very cold. Strain into the prepared rocks glass with fresh ice. Garnish with a wedge of lime.

Make & Muddle Spicy Margarita

Glass: Rocks
Served: On the rocks
Yield: 1 drink

2 oz. blanco tequila
1–1½ oz. Make & Muddle 2 Pepper Agave (or substitute; see chapter 4)
1–1½ oz. citrus mix (equal parts lemon, lime, and orange juice)
Lime wedges for glass prep and garnish

Prepare the glass by running a lime wedge around the rim and then dipping the rim into a mixture of 1 cup sugar and 1 tbsp. kosher salt. Add the ingredients to a cocktail shaker with ice. Shake until very cold. Strain into the prepared rocks glass with fresh ice. Garnish with a wedge of lime.

Bitter Blood

Glass: Rocks
Served: On the rocks
Yield: 1 drink

1 oz. tequila
¾ oz. Amara Amaro d'Arancia Rossa
1 oz. blood orange juice
½ oz. Make & Muddle 2 Pepper Agave (or substitute; see chapter 4)
Lime wedges for glass prep and garnish

Prepare the glass by running a lime wedge around the rim and then dipping the rim into either Tajín or a mixture of 1 cup sugar and 1 tbsp. kosher salt. Tajín can be found at most grocery stores in the produce section. Add the ingredients to a cocktail shaker with ice. Shake until very cold. Strain into the prepared rocks glass with fresh ice. Garnish with a wedge of lime.

Watermelon Margarita

Glass: Rocks
Served: On the rocks
Yield: 1 drink

2 oz. blanco tequila
1 cup cubed watermelon, seeds removed
1 oz. Make & Muddle 2 Pepper Agave (or substitute; see chapter 4)
½ oz. lime juice
½ oz. water
Watermelon cube for garnish

Add the watermelon to a blender or food processor and process until very smooth. Strain the solids out and use the remaining watermelon juice in the recipe, approximately ½ cup. Alternatively, muddle 4 or 5 cubes of watermelon in the bottom of the cocktail shaker before adding the other ingredients. Add the ingredients to a cocktail shaker with ice and shake until very cold. Strain into a rocks glass with fresh ice. Garnish with a cube of watermelon on a pick.

"I have plans for you, my fellow cocktail evangelists—plans for delicious cocktails that are blessedly batchable and will restore your hope and faith in cocktails made by the pitcher"

Egg Whites

Traditionally, whiskey sour recipes include an egg white. The egg white can round out the edges of an inferior spirit, taking away its harsh characteristics. It also adds body to the cocktail, giving it a frothy head and a silky smooth mouthfeel. Whether to use an egg white is entirely up to you, but I recommend trying it at least once.

You don't have to use raw egg whites to achieve these results. Powdered egg white added to the shaker works well. It is shelf stable and easy to measure, and there is no chance of contracting a food-borne illness.

If you do use an egg white or egg white substitute, there are two shaking techniques. To achieve the frothiest cocktail, I start with a "dry shake": add all the ingredients to the shaker without ice and shake for 30 seconds to aerate and emulsify the cocktail. Then add ice and shake again—the "wet shake." Alternatively, you could dry-shake the cocktail as the last step, but dry-shaking first results in a smoother foam because emulsification and aeration work best in a warm environment.

A word of warning when dry-shaking cocktails: due to the lack of ice, the shaker contents will expand (whereas ice causes the contents to contract). Inevitably, the shaker will spit at you when you open it after the dry shake. Just be prepared for that mini cocktail baptism, and don't wear your Sunday best.

The Whiskey Sour

Glass: Coupe
Served: Up
Yield: 1 drink

2 oz. bourbon
1 oz. fresh lemon juice
1 oz. simple syrup
Egg white
Aromatic bitters for garnish

Add the ingredients to a dry shaker. Shake for 30 seconds. Add ice to the shaker and shake again until very cold. Strain into a coupe glass. Garnish with a few drops of aromatic bitters.

The Make & Muddle Whiskey Sour

Glass: Coupe
Served: Up
Yield: 1 drink

2 oz. bourbon
1 oz. fresh lemon juice
1 oz. Make & Muddle 7 Syrup (or substitute; see chapter 4)
Egg white (optional)
Lemon peel for garnish

Add the ingredients to a shaker with ice. Shake until very cold. Strain into a coupe glass. Garnish with a lemon peel.

Maple Leaf

Glass: Rocks
Served: On the rocks
Yield: 1 drink

2 oz. bourbon
1 oz. fresh lemon juice
½–¾ oz. maple syrup
Dash aromatic bitters
Lemon peel for garnish

Add the ingredients to a shaker with ice. Shake until very cold. Strain into a rocks glass with fresh ice. Garnish with lemon peel.

Decorative Gourd Season

Glass: Coupe or martini
Served: On the rocks
Yield: 1 drink

2 oz. bourbon
1 oz. apple cider reduction
¾ oz. fresh lemon juice
¾ oz. Cynar
½ oz. Make & Muddle 7 Syrup (or substitute; see chapter 4)
Dash molasses bitters
Lightly salted apple slice for garnish

Add the ingredients to a cocktail shaker with ice. Shake until very cold. Strain onto fresh ice in a coupe or martini glass. Garnish with a salted apple slice.

Gimlets

The gimlet is a variety of sour that uses gin as the spirit. The basic recipe is gin, lime juice, and sugar. By playing with the sweet and sour elements, you can elevate your gimlet and make it playful and fresh or moody and complex, depending on how you flavor the syrup. The basil gimlet is my favorite summer gimlet. I muddle the basil in the shaker for extra depth.

Basil Gimlet

Glass: Coupe
Served: Up
Yield: 1 drink

Fresh basil leaves
Lime wedge
1½ oz. gin
¾ oz. basil syrup (see the recipe in chapter 4)
¾ oz. lime juice
Basil leaf for garnish

Muddle several fresh basil leaves with a lime wedge in a cocktail shaker. Add the remaining ingredients to the cocktail shaker with ice. Shake for about 20 seconds or until very cold. Double-strain into a chilled coupe glass or martini glass. Garnish with a basil leaf.

Peach Basil Gimlet

Glass: Coupe or martini
Served: Up
Yield: 1 drink

Half a peach
Fresh basil leaves
Lime wedge
1½ oz. gin
¾ oz. basil syrup (see the recipe in chapter 4)
¾ oz. lime juice
Basil leaf or peach slice for garnish

Muddle the peach half and a few fresh basil leaves with a lime wedge in a cocktail shaker. Add the remaining ingredients to the cocktail shaker with ice. Shake for about 20 seconds or until very cold. Double-strain into a chilled coupe glass or martini glass. Garnish with a basil leaf or slice of peach.

3 Herb Gracious Grapefruit Gimlet

Glass: Coupe
Served: Up
Yield: 1 drink

2 oz. barrel-aged gin
¾ oz. Make & Muddle 3 Herb Gracious Grapefruit Syrup (or substitute; see chapter 4)
½ oz. grapefruit juice
½ oz. lime juice

Add the ingredients to a cocktail shaker with ice. Shake and strain into a chilled coupe glass.

Chartreuse is a liqueur created in France in 1840. It contains more than 130 "plant substances" consisting of bark, roots, spices, and flowers. It has a strong vegetal quality and is an amazing ingredient in a cocktail. It is still produced in France and is available in yellow and green varieties (I like the yellow).

The Last Word Heard

Glass: Coupe
Served: Up
Yield: 1 drink

1 oz. gin
1 oz. lime juice
1 oz. yellow Chartreuse
1 oz. Make & Muddle Spiced Cherry Vanilla Syrup (or substitute; see chapter 4)
Cherry for garnish

Add the ingredients to a cocktail shaker with ice. Shake until very cold. Strain into a chilled coupe glass. Garnish with a cherry.

Sour Plus Bubbles

Over the years, I have experimented with lots of "bubbles" to top a cocktail—from seltzers to prosecco and everything in between. Adding a carbonated liquid of any kind changes a cocktail in some fun ways. Diluting a cocktail opens up its flavors and notes and gives it a little room to breathe. Plus, it's just fun to drink fizzy things. My general rule is that if a cocktail has lots of intense flavors and needs room to breathe, I add a seltzer. If I want bubbles without much dilution, I add prosecco or champagne. Go forth and top your cocktails with bubbles.

Lavender 75

Glass: Champagne flute
Served: Up
Yield: 1 drink

1½ oz. vodka or gin
¾ oz. Make & Muddle Honey Lavender Elixir (or substitute; see chapter 4)
¾ oz. fresh lemon juice
Prosecco
Lemon twist for garnish

Add the vodka or gin, Honey Lavender Elixir, and lemon juice to a cocktail shaker with ice. Shake until very cold. Strain into a champagne flute. Top with prosecco. Garnish with a lemon twist.

Freya's Tears

Glass: Champagne flute
Served: Up
Yield: 1 drink

1½ oz. aquavit
¾ oz. Make & Muddle 3 Herb Gracious Grapefruit Syrup (or substitute; see chapter 4)
½ oz. grapefruit juice
¼ oz. fresh lemon juice
3 sprigs fresh thyme (1 for garnish)
Prosecco

Add the aquavit, syrup, fruit juices, and 2 sprigs of thyme to a cocktail shaker with ice. Shake until very cold. Strain into a champagne flute. Top with prosecco. Garnish with a thyme sprig.

8

MARTINIS

Foundation ingredients: gin, vermouth

There is nothing as iconic as a martini. If I never make another cocktail, I will lack for nothing, as the martini is utter perfection. It is the way and the truth. What comes after this cocktail has not yet appeared, but we know that when it does, it will be divine.

If a cocktail could embody a lifestyle, the martini is the one I want to have—simple, elegant, and spirit forward. Cocktail history tells us that the martini is descended from a very early cocktail called the Martinez, consisting of Old Tom gin, sweet vermouth, Maraschino liqueur, and aromatic bitters. This cocktail was named for its place of origin near Martinez, California. Rumor has it that the Martinez is a direct descendant of the Manhattan. In 1888 *The New and Improved Illustrated Bartender's Manual* was published with a typo that changed the Martinez to the "Martine." It was a short hop from Martine to martini.

Old Tom gin was popular before Prohibition. It used more than the usual amount of malt in its grain recipe (mash bill), which added body and depth of flavor. During Prohibition, Old Tom virtually disappeared from American bar shelves and was replaced by London dry gin.

Another step in the martini's evolution involves a decrease in the popularity of vermouth and its lack of quality. Vermouth is a wonderful fortified wine that can be very enjoyable on its own. However, many US bars opt for inexpensive vermouth and then fail to store it properly. Vermouth should be treated like a bottle of wine and refrigerated after opening. So it's no mystery why the amount of vermouth in the standard martini recipe has been reduced to a drop or two. The average American bar eliminates vermouth from the vodka martini altogether.

A martini can be served up or on the rocks, although up is the default option. It can be garnished with an olive, possibly stuffed with cheese or garlic, or with a twist of lemon.

Shaking versus Stirring

Shaking incorporates air into a cocktail. One result is that certain elements evaporate, including some of the lighter aromas found in spirits. When these lighter aromas evaporate, mid and base aromas are left behind, totally changing the profile the distiller intended when making the gin. In this case, shaking can create an unbalanced cocktail. This is more perceptible in a cocktail with few ingredients, especially if the ingredients are primarily spirits.

That being said, I recommend stirring martinis, especially if you're using one of the dozens of delicious craft gins on the market. An exception to the stirring rule is the vodka martini. Vodka is a neutral spirit, so shaking has less of an impact on its flavor profile. Plus, many vodka martini drinkers prefer their cocktails frosty cold with ice crystals in the cocktail, and shaking is an efficient and effective way to achieve a martini that would make the angels weep.

Wet, Dry, Very Dry, or Dirty

A classic martini recipe is 4–5 parts spirit and 1 part vermouth. A "wet" martini has more vermouth, and a "dry" martini has less vermouth. A "very dry" martini has only a splash of vermouth. A good friend of mine who loves her martinis very dry instructs the bartender to "just show the vermouth to the gin." A "dirty" martini is a classic martini with olive brine added.

Chilled Glassware, or How to Keep That Cocktail Cold

Stemware is not just about aesthetics. There is a function to its form. When we consume cocktails out of stemware, we are meant to hold the stem instead of the bowl of the glass so that our hands do not warm the cocktail. For anything I serve up, I like to chill the glass before I pour the cocktail: either add ice water to the glass while building the cocktail or simply store the glasses in the freezer.

Classic Gin Martini

Glass: Martini or coupe
Served: Up
Yield: 1 drink

2 oz. London dry gin
½ oz. dry vermouth
Lemon twist or olives for garnish

Chill the glass as you mix the cocktail. Add the ingredients to a mixing glass with ice. Stir until very cold. Strain into the chilled glass. Garnish with a lemon twist or olives.

Dry & Dirty Vodka Martini

Glass: Martini or coupe
Served: Up
Yield: 1 drink

2 oz. vodka
Spritz of vermouth
¼ oz. olive brine
Lemon twist or olives for garnish

Chill the glass as you mix the cocktail. Add the ingredients to a mixing glass with ice. Stir until very cold. Strain into the chilled glass. Garnish with a lemon twist or olives.

"If I never make another cocktail, I will lack for nothing, as the martini is utter perfection."

Make & Muddle Lemon Drop

Glass: Martini or coupe
Served: Up
Yield: 1 drink

3 oz. vodka
¾ oz. fresh lemon juice
¾ oz. Make & Muddle Honey Lavender
Elixir (or substitute; see chapter 4)
Lemon twist for garnish

Chill the glass as you mix the cocktail. Add
the ingredients to a mixing glass with ice.
Stir until very cold. Strain into the chilled
glass. Garnish with a lemon twist.

Espresso Martini

Glass: Martini or coupe
Served: Up
Yield: 1 drink

2 oz. vodka or vanilla vodka
1 oz. coffee liqueur
1 oz. espresso, freshly brewed (or cold-brew
concentrate)
3 coffee beans for garnish

Chill the glass as you mix the cocktail. Add
the ingredients to a shaker with ice and
shake until very cold. Strain into the chilled
glass. Garnish with coffee beans.

"Shaking is an efficient and
effective way to achieve a
martini that would make
the angels weep."

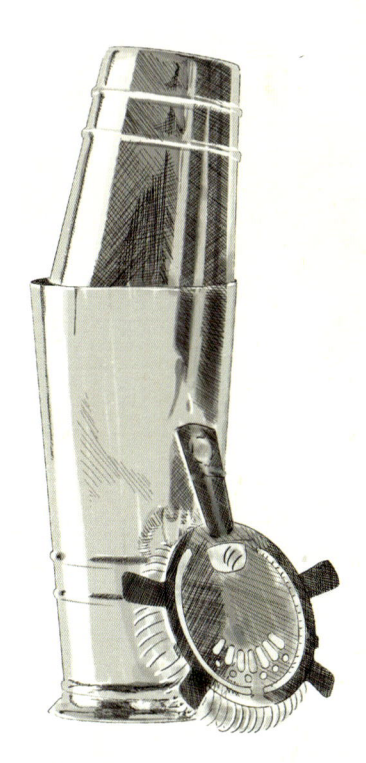

The Cosmopolitan

There are so many origin stories that it's impossible to figure out who really invented the Cosmopolitan. What we know for sure is that the Kamikaze cocktail—basically a vodka gimlet with vodka, lime juice, and orange curaçao—was popular around the mid-twentieth century. Someone added a splash of cranberry juice, and the Cosmo was born. Fast-forward to *Sex and the City* and Carrie Bradshaw's drink of choice, and the Cosmo's popularity skyrocketed.

In the 1990s I was enjoying the carefree single life of a twenty-something. I lived in the downstairs of a duplex, and my upstairs neighbor became a good friend. If there was anything we loved more than ice cold champagne it was a well-made Cosmopolitan. We made it our mission to tour the best bars and restaurants in the city and challenge the bartenders: "We are on a mission to find the very best Cosmo in the city. Are you up for the challenge?" They were. We drank our fair share of Cosmos that year, and I have no regrets. This exhaustive experiment also led to a damn fine recipe.

Cosmopolitan

Glass: Martini or coupe
Served: Up
Yield: 1 drink

2 oz. vodka
1 oz. cranberry juice
½ oz. orange curaçao
½ oz. lime juice
Orange twist for garnish

Chill the glass while you build the cocktail. Add the ingredients to a cocktail shaker with ice. Shake until very cold. Strain into the chilled glass. Garnish with an orange twist.

"If there was anything we loved more than ice cold champagne it was a well-made Cosmopolitan."

Urbane Equinox

Glass: Coupe
Served: Up
Yield: 1 drink

2 oz. vodka or gin
2 oz. Make & Muddle Orange Ginger
Cranberry Shrub (or substitute; see chapter 4)
Splash fresh lime juice
Lime or lemon twist, cranberry, or rosemary
sprig for garnish

Chill the glass. Add the ingredients to a
shaker full of ice. Shake to chill and strain
into the chilled glass. Garnish with a lime or
lemon twist, a cranberry, or a rosemary sprig.

Tequila Martini

Glass: Martini or coupe
Served: Up
Yield: 1 drink

2 oz. reposado tequila, preferably 100
percent blue Weber agave highlands tequila
¼ oz. good-quality dry vermouth
Olive brine for rinsing the glass
2 olives for garnish

Chill the glass. Add the tequila and
vermouth to a mixing glass with ice. Stir
until very cold. Pour enough olive brine into
the chilled glass to coat the inside. Strain
the martini into the glass and garnish with
olives.

**"If a cocktail could embody
a lifestyle, the martini is the
one I want to have—simple,
elegant, and spirit forward."**

9

HIGHBALLS

Foundation ingredients: spirit, nonalcoholic mixer

Brothers and sisters, whatsoever things are true, whatsoever things are honest, whatsoever things are just, whatsoever things are pure, whatsoever things are lovely, whatsoever things are of good report; if there be any virtue, and if there be any praise—it is surely the highball.

Technically, a highball is any cocktail in which a nonalcoholic mixer plays a bigger part than the alcoholic spirit. This is a broad and inclusive category that includes the simple gin and tonic and the bourbon rickey. But one of my favorite highball cocktails is also one of the most labor intensive: the mojito. Most bartenders hate to make this cocktail because muddling takes time, and it's tough to do it justice when the bar is busy. But that's not an issue at your home bar.

During one of my trips to the Caribbean, I had a mojito that changed my life. Prior to that, every mojito I ever drank was terrible—sickly sweet, flat, and watered down. But this one was exotic, slightly fizzy, and tart; it was minty magic in a glass sweating from the coldness of the cocktail. The taste was like nothing I had ever experienced, and I was hooked. At first, I thought maybe it was just an island thing. Or maybe I was sun drunk from too much salt water and sand. Scuba diving does tend to make me slightly loopy. But no; this mojito was that good.

After that trip, I became deeply devoted to perfecting the mojito. The most important tip I can offer is that every ingredient that goes into this drink should be as cold as possible. I store bottles of rum in the freezer during the summer for this very reason. Warm liquor instantly dilutes the drink, especially if you are building it in the serving glass instead of a separate mixing glass, as is traditional with the mojito. Don't take shortcuts on this cocktail. I promise it will be worth the effort. And you can rest on the beach when you're done.

The Mojito

Glass: Tom Collins or tumbler
Served: On the rocks
Yield: 1 drink

3 oz. cold silver rum
¼ cup fresh mint, loosely packed
2 heaping tsp. organic sugar
4 lime wedges (1 for garnish)
Cold sparkling water or club soda
Fresh mint for garnish

In the serving glass, muddle the mint, sugar, and 3 lime wedges until the sugar has dissolved and the mint and lime are bruised but not crushed. Add ice to the glass, add rum and sparkling water, and stir. Garnish with the last lime wedge and fresh mint.

> **"Exotic, slightly fizzy, and tart; it was minty magic in a glass sweating from the coldness of the cocktail. . . . This mojito was that good."**

Make & Muddle
Bourbon Rickey

Glass: Rocks
Served: On the rocks
Yield: 1 drink

1½ oz. bourbon
1 oz. Make & Muddle 3 Herb Gracious
Grapefruit Syrup (or substitute; see chapter 4)
½ oz. lime juice
Seltzer or Lime High Noon
Lime wedge or grapefruit peel for garnish

Add the bourbon, syrup, and lime juice to
a cocktail shaker with ice. Shake until very
cold. Strain into a rocks glass with fresh ice.
Top with seltzer or Lime High Noon. Garnish
with a wedge of lime or grapefruit peel.

A Pair of Mules

I am always intrigued by a recipe that translates from one liquor to another. Some spirits make the transition seamlessly (brandy to bourbon), but others couldn't be farther apart (vodka to bourbon). When the Kentucky mule (made with bourbon) became the unofficial drink of summer some years ago, I decided to try the original Moscow mule (made with vodka). Each spirit did drastically different things, as expected, but both were equally delicious. Bourbon is a much sweeter spirit than vodka, so there is less ginger beer and more tart lime in that mule.

The traditional glassware for a mule is a copper mug, but don't be deceived, my fellow evangelists. This was a marketing ploy. The mule's hazy cocktail history takes us back to 1941, when John Martin, president of the Heublein spirits company, was trying to promote Smirnoff to folks who were largely uninterested in a Russian-sounding vodka. He met up with Jack Morgan, owner of the Cock'n Bull pub on Hollywood's Sunset Strip, who made a ginger beer that imbibers were indifferent to. The two of them (along with a girlfriend who was selling copper mugs, if you believe the legend) teamed up to create a cocktail that immediately appealed to the Hollywood crowd. Mules are still one of the most popular highball cocktails. Although the copper mug is traditional, it has nothing to do with keeping the beverage cold. Ceramic glassware actually holds the cold longer than a copper mug. You are welcome to serve these mules however you like.

Moscow Mule

Glass: Copper mug or ceramic cup
Served: On the rocks
Yield: 1 drink

3 oz. cold vodka
3 oz. cold ginger beer
2 lime wedges (1 for garnish)
¼ cup fresh mint, loosely packed
Sprig of fresh mint for garnish

In a copper mug or ceramic cup, muddle 1 lime wedge and the mint together. Add ice and pour the vodka and ginger beer over the ice. Stir to combine the ingredients. Top with a lime wedge and sprig of mint.

Kentucky Mule

Glass: Copper mug or ceramic cup
Served: On the rocks
Yield: 1 drink

3 oz. cold bourbon
2 oz. cold ginger beer
½ oz. fresh lime juice
2 lime wedges (1 for garnish)
¼ cup fresh mint, loosely packed
Sprig of fresh mint for garnish

In a copper mug or ceramic cup, muddle 1 lime wedge and the mint together. Add ice and pour the bourbon, ginger beer, and lime juice over the ice. Stir to combine the ingredients. Top with a lime wedge and sprig of mint.

Make & Muddle
Spiced Cherry Highball

Glass: Rocks
Served: On the rocks
Yield: 1 drink

1½ oz. rum
1 oz. Make & Muddle Spiced Cherry Vanilla
Syrup (or substitute; see chapter 4)
¼ oz. lime juice
Lime seltzer or Lime High Noon
Cherry for garnish

Add the rum, syrup, and lime juice to a
shaker with ice. Shake until very cold. Strain
into a rocks glass with fresh ice. Top with
lime seltzer or Lime High Noon. Garnish
with a cherry.

**"If there be any virtue, and
if there be any praise—it is
surely the highball."**

10

NEGRONIS

Foundation ingredients: gin, Campari, sweet vermouth

This lovely cocktail's history begins at Bar Casoni in Florence, Italy, circa 1919. I will be glad and rejoice; I will sing the praises of the Italian nobleman Count Camillo Negroni. He invented the cocktail when he had bartender Forsco Scarselli make an Americano (Campari, vermouth, and sparkling water) with gin instead of sparkling water. The count made the cocktail immensely popular, and then his family created a distillery that sold a ready-to-drink version called Antico Negroni. The distillery is still in operation today.

Campari is an aperitif that is both bitter and sweet. Some would call it an acquired taste. For those of us who love it, we must go out and make disciples. The Negroni is Campari at its finest.

Campari will always remind me of Italy, and I drank my fair share of Negronis when I was there. One in particular stands out. I was at a lakeside restaurant on Lake Como. It was June, and the heat was already miserable. I sat down in the cool of the shade and ordered a cocktail. It came to the table looking like salvation and tasting like sin—bitter, sweet, and boozy, yet completely refreshing. It remains one of my favorite cocktails, and I regularly order Negronis when I'm out and make them at home too.

This cocktail has a 1:1:1 ratio, meaning equal parts gin, vermouth, and Campari. I like mine with more spirit, so I use a 2:1:1 ratio. Try it both ways and see which you prefer. The Negroni is traditionally served up, but I like it on a big rock. In addition to the dilution, which I like, the ice helps you sip slowly. This cocktail is one that can go down very quickly.

The Negroni

Glass: Rocks
Served: On the rocks
Yield: 1 drink

2 oz. gin
1 oz. Campari
1 oz. sweet vermouth (I prefer Antica)
Lemon peel for garnish

Add the ingredients to a mixing glass with ice. Stir until very cold. Strain onto a big rock and garnish with a lemon peel.

"I sat down in the cool of the shade and ordered a cocktail. It came to the table looking like salvation and tasting like sin."

The Boulevardier was invented in Paris at Harry's New York Bar in the 1920s. This delicious cocktail was rumored to be the signature drink of expatriate writer Erskine Gwynne, a trendsetting socialite and nephew of railroad tycoon Alfred Vanderbilt. Gwynne published a magazine in Paris called *The Boulevardier*. It took some years for the cocktail to make its way to America, but once it did, it became a classic.

The Boulevardier

Glass: Rocks
Served: On the rocks
Yield: 1 drink

2 oz. bourbon
1 oz. Campari
1 oz. sweet vermouth
Orange peel for garnish

Add the ingredients to a mixing glass with ice. Stir until very cold. Strain onto a big rock and garnish with an orange peel.

The Negroni Sbagliato was a happy accident. Somehow, a bartender botched a Negroni by adding sparkling wine instead of gin, creating a refreshing, spritz-like cocktail.

Negroni Sbagliato

Glass: Rocks or champagne flute
Served: On the rocks or up
Yield: 1 drink

1 oz. Campari
1 oz. sweet vermouth
Prosecco
Lemon peel or wheel for garnish

Add the Campari and vermouth to the serving glass. Add ice (if you like), top with prosecco, and garnish with a lemon peel or lemon wheel.

The Cardinale

Glass: Rocks
Served: On the rocks
Yield: 1 drink

2 oz. gin
1 oz. Campari
1 oz. dry vermouth
Lemon peel for garnish

Add the ingredients to a mixing glass with ice. Stir until very cold. Strain onto a big rock and garnish with a lemon peel.

If day drinking is wrong, I don't want to be right, especially if there's time for an afternoon nap. The Buongiorno is my take on a brunch Boulevardier. The addition of cold-brew coffee elevates this drink to one that wakes you up as it boozes you up.

Buongiorno

Glass: Rocks
Served: On the rocks
Yield: 1 drink

1½ oz. bourbon
1½ oz. Aperol
3 oz. cold-brew coffee
Dash orange bitters
Dash Peychaud's bitters
Orange peel for garnish

Add the ingredients to a mixing glass with ice. Stir until very cold. Strain into a rocks glass with one large ice cube. Garnish with an orange peel.

11

TODDIES

*Foundation ingredients: spirit (whiskey, brandy, rum),
lemon, honey, hot water*

Brothers and sisters, we recognize the ancient wisdom in giving strong drink to those who are perishing, and wine to those who are bitter of heart. This is still sound advice! Alcohol has always been considered medicinal. The ancient Egyptians mixed herbs with wine to make medicine, and Parisians used absinthe to treat intestinal worms. Bourbon distilleries were allowed to remain open during Prohibition to produce "medicinal alcohol." Alcohol has always been used to do more than alter our moods.

Toddies fall into this category. The toddy started in British-controlled India in the 1610s. The Hindi word *taddy* means a "beverage made from fermented palm sap." By 1786, the taddy was officially defined as a "beverage made of alcoholic liquor with hot water, sugar, and spices." The British then brought the drink home and made it truly British with the addition of a distilled spirit such as brandy or whiskey. The cold and damp of Great Britain cry out for something hot and boozy to warm you up.

"The toddy is an iconic cocktail and certainly has medicinal properties that we are happy to partake in."

It has also been rumored that the toddy originated in Dublin when a physician named Robert Bentley Todd prescribed a mixture of brandy, cinnamon, sugar, and hot water to his patients. Regardless of its origin, the toddy is an iconic cocktail and certainly has medicinal properties that we are happy to partake in.

The Hot Toddy

Glass: Mug or footed glass
Served: Hot
Yield: 1 drink

1½ oz. whiskey, brandy, or dark rum
1 tbsp. honey
¼–½ oz. fresh lemon juice
Hot water
Lemon wheel for garnish

Add the ingredients to a mug and stir to combine. Garnish with a lemon wheel.

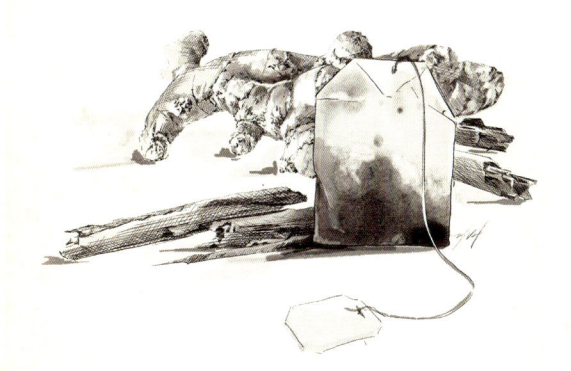

Hot Whiskey Toddy

Glass: Mug or footed glass
Served: Hot
Yield: 1 drink

1½ oz. bourbon
1½ oz. toddy syrup (recipe follows)
1 oz. lemon juice
Boiling water
Lemon wedge or peel for garnish

Add the bourbon, syrup, and lemon juice to a mug. Top with boiling water and garnish with a lemon wedge or peel.

Toddy Syrup

1 cup water
1 cup sugar
2 black tea bags
¾ cup grated ginger
Zest of 1 lemon
½ cup honey

Bring water to a boil and add sugar, stirring until dissolved. Add tea bags, ginger, and lemon zest. Stir gently. Remove from heat and add honey. Stir to mix. Steep for 30 minutes and remove tea bags. Steep another 1½ hours. Strain and squeeze the solids to get all the syrup.

When you hear the words *gin* and *toddy* in the same sentence, you probably want to run in the other direction. But the combination of gin and citrus juices makes a wonderful toddy. Try it once and you will be a believer. I actually prefer a gin toddy to a whiskey toddy, but don't tell anyone. I would lose my bourbon street cred if they knew.

Gin Toddy

Glass: Mug or footed glass
Served: Hot
Yield: 1 drink

1½ oz. gin
1 oz. fresh grapefruit juice
¾ oz. Make & Muddle Honey Lavender Elixir (or substitute; see chapter 4)
¼ oz. fresh lemon juice
Boiling water
Lemon or grapefruit wedge or peel for garnish

Add the first 4 ingredients to a mug. Top with boiling water and garnish with a lemon or grapefruit wedge or peel.

Tequila Toddy

Glass: Mug or footed glass
Served: Hot
Yield: 1 drink

3 oz. hot water
Chamomile tea bag
1½ oz. reposado or añejo tequila
½ oz. Make & Muddle 2 Pepper Agave Syrup (or substitute; see chapter 4)
½ oz. lemon juice

In a mug, steep the tea bag in the hot water. Add the remaining ingredients and stir.

Brandy Toddy

Glass: Mug or footed glass
Served: Hot
Yield: 1 drink

1½ oz. brandy
½ oz. apple brandy
½ oz. Make & Muddle 7 Syrup (or substitute; see chapter 4)
½ oz. lemon juice
Hot water
Cinnamon stick for garnish

Add the ingredients to a mug and stir. Garnish with a cinnamon stick.

Mulled Wine

Warm and medicinal cocktails don't have to be spirit based. Mulled wine reportedly originated in the second century, when the Romans drank this warm libation to help them withstand the cold winters. Europeans mixed heated wine with spices because of the supposed medicinal value. They also used herbs and flowers as natural sweeteners to make harsh, inexpensive wines more palatable.

Like many trendy cocktails, the popularity of mulled wine faded, except in Sweden. Perhaps the Swedes gravitated toward tasty, warm alcoholic beverages because of the climate. The Swedish monarchy made several variations of mulled wine famous over the centuries. As more recipes were created, recipe books and writings started to refer to mulled wine as glögg, which was first mentioned in 1609. Glögg became associated with Christmas in the 1890s, when the popularity of the warm, spiced wine skyrocketed. Wine merchants across Sweden had their own unique recipes, which were distributed throughout the rest of Europe.

We love mulled wine during the winter months, holidays or not. It is the perfect beverage on a cold night in front of the fire. It is also the perfect festive cocktail to batch for a party and let guests serve themselves throughout the evening. If there happen to be leftovers, they store beautifully in the refrigerator for up to a week.

Mulled Wine

Glass: Mug or footed glass
Served: Hot
Yield: 1 drink

6 oz. full-bodied red wine
½ oz. bourbon
1 oz. Make & Muddle 7 Syrup (or substitute; see chapter 4)
½ oz. lemon juice
Lemon and orange wedges for garnish

Add the ingredients to a mug. Stir and microwave to the desired temperature. Garnish with lemon and orange wedges.

To make a batch, mix 1 bottle red wine, ½ cup bourbon, 2–3 oz. 7 Syrup, and 2 oz. lemon juice in an electric cooking pot. Set the pot on low and enjoy throughout the evening.

"Glögg became associated with Christmas in the 1890s, when the popularity of the warm, spiced wine skyrocketed."

12

SPRITZES AND SANGRIAS

Sparkling Wine

I couldn't start a chapter on spritzes without first mentioning sparkling wine, known in my house simply as "bubbles." We drink a little wine for the stomach and our infirmities. We eat with joy and drink our wine with a merry heart. Oh, how it sparkles in the cup! Oh, how my heart and mind rejoice to think of those tiny bubbles (the smaller the better)!

When I was in my twenties, my mom, my sister, and I took one of our annual girls' trips to Chicago, where we stayed at an extravagant hotel, went shopping, ate and drank all kinds of wonderful things, and ordered room service dessert and coffee in our pajamas. We saved all year for these utterly decadent trips. One night, we were talking disparagingly about a restaurant that had served us warm champagne when my mother turned to us and said, "Girls, I have some life lessons to tell you." Thinking she was about to impart her deepest heartfelt secrets, we leaned in. She said, "Please, for all that is good and holy, remember that vodka and champagne have to be served ice cold." We devolved into a fit of laughter but have absolutely taken that advice to heart.

Sparkling wines are region specific. Champagne—the queen of all sparkling wines, in my opinion—is made in the Champagne region of France using the *méthode traditionnelle*. The wine is first fermented in a barrel. Then, when it is bottled, small amounts of sugar and yeast are added, and a second fermentation occurs, producing alcohol and carbon dioxide. Once the bottle is capped, the carbon dioxide is forced into the wine and creates the bubbles we all adore. The bottles are stored on their sides, and as the yeast ferments the sugar, it clumps together and collects on the sides of the bottles. The bottles are turned slightly every day, which causes the spent yeast to collect at the top of the bottle. This process is called riddling.

Once all the sugar is fermented and all the yeast has collected at the top of the bottle, the tip of the bottle containing the yeast sediment is frozen, the cap is removed, and the frozen yeast is expelled by the pressure from the now carbonated wine. This process is known as disgorging.

In the final step of the process, a mixture of sugar and finished champagne (called dosage) is added to replace the volume of disgorged yeast. The amount of dosage differs. The sweetest champagnes are labeled doux, followed by demi-sec, dry, extra dry, brut, and extra brut. If no dosage is added, the champagne is labeled brut zero or brut nature.

The *méthode traditionnelle* can be followed by vintners anywhere. For example, Cava is a Spanish sparkling wine made with this method. Wine made in France outside of the Champagne region that follows the *méthode traditionnelle* is frequently called Crémant. For example, Crémant de Loire is made mostly from Chenin Blanc in the Loire Valley.

Prosecco, the sparkling wine traditionally used in spritzes, is produced in northern Italy. It is made from mostly Glera grapes but may include other varietals such as Pinot Grigio, Chardonnay, Pinot Bianco, and Pinot Noir. Proseccos can vary in sweetness from dry to extra dry to brut. They are often less expensive than champagne but are absolutely delicious. I have found that it's easier to find a good inexpensive prosecco than a good inexpensive champagne.

The Spritz

Foundation ingredients: prosecco, bitter liqueur, soda water

The spritz originated in Venice at the end of the nineteenth century, when Venice was still part of the Austrian Empire. Soldiers stationed there drank the local wines but added a *Spritz* (German for "splash.") to the wine to lower the alcohol content and make it similar to the beer they were used to drinking. The original spritz consisted of equal parts white wine and soda water.

In Veneto (the northeastern region of Italy where Venice is located), the Spritz al Bitter was created by adding a bitter liqueur in a ratio of 3:2:1—3 parts prosecco, 2 parts bitter liqueur (commonly Campari or Aperol), 1 part soda water. This easy ratio lends itself to improvisation if you have a few bitter liqueurs on hand.

One of the most iconic qualities of the spritz is its understated elegance: three ingredients swimming in a wine goblet full of ice with beads of sweat dripping down the side and topped with a lavish garnish. The spritz is the official cocktail of Italy, and rightly so. Italy has created the spritz for those of us who need some elegance. It is also my official cocktail as the weather starts to warm and before mint julep season begins.

The Italian Spritz

Glass: Large wine goblet
Served: On the rocks
Yield: 1 drink

3 oz. prosecco
2 oz. Campari or Aperol
1 oz. soda water
Large orange wheel for garnish

Fill a wine goblet with ice and add the ingredients. Stir gently until combined. Garnish with a large orange wheel.

When I was in Italy before the pandemic, I drank my way through the country one spritz at a time. I experienced one particularly magical day in Rome, where I did a "progressive evening" of a cocktail and a nosh at the best hotel rooftops. On a whim, my travel companion and I ended up at the Hotel Eden's Michelin star restaurant La Terrazza. We had no reservations and no idea what to expect, just a recommendation from our wonderful Airbnb host. What we got was a stunning view of Rome as the sun was setting and sublime food and cocktails. The restaurant's gorgeous Hugo Spritz came to me in a glass garnished with a large sprig of fresh, fragrant mint. Following is

the recipe for the original Hugo Spritz and the Make & Muddle version. The splash of Honey Lavender Elixir softens the gin and brightens the Cynar. Saluti!

Hugo Spritz

Glass: Large wine goblet
Served: On the rocks
Yield: 1 drink

3 oz. prosecco
1½ oz. Cynar
1½ oz. gin
1 oz. seltzer
Fresh mint and lemon wheel for garnish

Build the cocktail in a large wine goblet with lots of ice.

Make & Muddle Hugo Spritz

Glass: Large wine goblet
Served: On the rocks
Yield: 1 drink

3 oz. prosecco
1½ oz. Cynar
1½ oz. gin
Splash Make & Muddle Honey Lavender Elixir (or substitute; see chapter 4)
1 oz. seltzer or lemon seltzer
Fresh mint and lemon wheel for garnish

Build the cocktail in a large wine goblet with lots of ice.

Make & Muddle Spiced Cherry Spritz

Glass: Large wine goblet
Served: On the rocks
Yield: 1 drink

2 oz. Amaro Averno
½ oz. Make & Muddle Spiced Cherry Vanilla Syrup (or substitute; see chapter 4)
3 oz. prosecco
Amarena cherry and lemon wheel for garnish

Build the cocktail in a large wine goblet with lots of ice.

"One of the most iconic qualities of the spritz is its understated elegance"

Sangria

Foundation ingredients: wine, spices and/or botanicals, sugar

Wine was probably the first alcoholic beverage. To make wine, all you have to do is let grape juice sit for a few days and allow the naturally occurring yeasts to do their work. Although you'll end up with wine, it won't necessarily be the highest quality. One way to cover up any undesirable attributes is to add other flavors.

Sangria, in one form or another, has existed since medieval times, when hippocras (a mulled wine) was enjoyed. Spices, water, and distilled spirits were added to wine and drunk by the urnful. The Romans took this beverage everywhere they colonized, including Spain, where it morphed into sangria. Sangria is essentially Spain's national beverage, and the name comes from the Spanish word for *blood*. Whether that refers to the red wine used in sangria or to what flows through many a Spaniard's veins is up to you to decide.

Traditionally, sangria calls for brandy, but I like what bourbon does with a good red wine. Sangria batches beautifully, which makes it perfect for gatherings when no one wants to tend bar.

Traditional Sangria

Glass: Pitcher for mixing; large wine goblet to serve
Served: On the rocks
Yield: 37 oz., or about 6 drinks

750 mL pinot noir
½ cup brandy
½ cup lemon juice
½ cup orange juice
½ cup simple syrup
Assorted fruit, cut up (e.g., lemons, limes, blueberries)
Edible flowers for garnish

Mix the ingredients in a large pitcher. Add ice. Garnish with edible flowers.

Make & Muddle Red Sangria

Glass: Pitcher for mixing; large wine goblet to serve
Served: On the rocks
Yield: 37 oz., or about 6 drinks

750 mL pinot noir
1 cup bourbon
½ cup lemon juice
¾ cup Make & Muddle 7 Syrup (or substitute; see chapter 4)
Assorted fruit, cut up (e.g., lemons, limes, blueberries)
Edible flowers for garnish

Mix the ingredients in a large pitcher. Add ice. Garnish with edible flowers.

Make & Muddle White Sangria

Glass: Pitcher for mixing; large wine goblet to serve
Served: On the rocks
Yield: 37 oz., or about 6 drinks

750 mL Moscato wine
4 oz. brandy
3 oz. Make & Muddle Honey Lavender Elixir (or substitute; see chapter 4)
½ cup citrus juice (equal parts lemon, lime, and orange juice)
Cut up fruit for garnish (e.g., lemons, limes, peaches, oranges)

Place the ingredients in a pitcher and stir. Garnish with fruit.

> "We eat with joy and drink our wine with a merry heart. Oh, how it sparkles in the cup! Oh, how my heart and mind rejoice to think of those tiny bubbles (the smaller the better)!"

13

Boozy Slushies

Grown-up slushies have become my weakness. I used to avoid slushies because they were so sweet I couldn't drink one without feeling nauseous halfway through it. Then I discovered that what I really wanted was something less sweet and topped with something fizzy. Be warned: this chapter will change your life. Friends, let the heavens rejoice, let the earth be glad: boozy slushies are here.

These beverages are perfect on a warm evening, but they can also be delicious, booze-soaked trouble—the kind of trouble where you stay up way past your bedtime to dance to 1980s power ballads with your friends. So clear your schedule and get ready for a good time. And for goodness' sake, remember to hydrate in between.

All the recipes here are batched because if I'm freezing cocktails, I might as well do it for a crowd. I use plastic quart-sized deli containers because they have lids, they stack well, and they don't take up too much space in the freezer. They are also the right size for a cooler if you need to transport them to the pool or the beach.

Island-Time Slush

Glass: Mix in a freezer-safe container with lid; serve in a rocks glass
Served: Frozen
Yield: About 1 quart

¾ cup dark rum
¾ cup coconut rum
1½ cups pineapple juice
½ cup Make & Muddle 2 Pepper Agave (or substitute; see chapter 4)
½ cup lime juice
½ cup water
Lime seltzer or lime hard seltzer to top

Mix all the ingredients (except the seltzer) in a freezer-safe container with a lid. Freeze for 24 hours, or until frozen. To serve, spoon the frozen slush into a glass and top with seltzer.

Make & Muddle Queen Bee Slush

Glass: Mix in a freezer-safe container with lid; serve in a rocks glass
Served: Frozen
Yield: About 1 quart

1½ cups vodka
¾ cup Make & Muddle Honey Lavender Elixir (or substitute; see chapter 4)
¾ cup lemon juice
¾ cup water
Seltzer or prosecco to top

Mix all the ingredients (except the seltzer or prosecco) in a freezer-safe container with a lid. Freeze for 24 hours, or until frozen. To serve, spoon the frozen slush into a glass and top with seltzer or prosecco.

"Be warned: this chapter will change your life. Friends, let the heavens rejoice, let the earth be glad: boozy slushies are here."

Make & Muddle Small-Town-Girl Slush

Glass: Mix in a freezer-safe container with lid; serve in a rocks glass
Served: Frozen
Yield: About 1 quart

1 cup vodka
1 cup Make & Muddle Honey Lavender Elixir (or substitute; see chapter 4)
¾ cup fresh grapefruit juice
½ cup lemon juice
½ cup water
Seltzer or prosecco to top

Mix all the ingredients (except the seltzer or prosecco) in a freezer-safe container with a lid. Freeze for 24 hours, or until frozen. To serve, spoon the frozen slush into a glass and top with seltzer or prosecco.

Bourbon Slush

Glass: Mix in a freezer-safe container with lid; serve in a rocks glass
Served: Frozen
Yield: About 1 gallon

5 cups brewed tea
4 cups orange juice
3 cups bourbon
1 cup Make & Muddle 7 Syrup (or substitute; see chapter 4)
1 cup water
½ cup fresh lemon juice
Prosecco, Sprite, or ginger ale to top
Orange slice or cherry for garnish

Mix the first 6 ingredients in a freezer-safe container with a lid. Freeze for 24 hours, or until frozen. To serve, fill a glass halfway with ice. Scoop the frozen slush into the glass and top with prosecco or with Sprite or ginger ale for a less boozy option. Garnish with an orange slice or cherry.

Blueberry Lemon Slush

Glass: Mix in a freezer-safe container with lid; serve in a tumbler
Served: Frozen
Yield: About 1 quart

24 oz. frozen blueberries
1 cup water
½ cup lemon juice
¼–⅓ cup maple syrup (according to taste)
Zest from 1 lemon
2 cups vodka or immature brandy
Prosecco to top
Blueberries and lemon twist for garnish

In a blender, process the blueberries, water, and lemon juice until very smooth (you may need to do this in batches). Strain the liquid through a fine mesh strainer into a 2-quart plastic container with a lid. Be sure to press on the blueberry solids to extract all the liquid. Add the maple syrup, lemon zest, and vodka to the strained juice. Stir to combine. Freeze for 24 hours, or until solid. To serve, scoop approximately ⅓ cup blueberry ice into a tumbler with ice. Top with prosecco and stir. Garnish with whole blueberries and a lemon twist.

> **"These beverages are perfect on a warm evening. . . . Stay up way past your bedtime to dance to 1980s power ballads with your friends."**

14

Spirit-Free Mocktails

Some people don't imbibe for one reason or another. And dry January has become a trend in recent years, when we just need a break from all the holiday food and booze. I firmly believe that there is a seat at the table for everyone whether they are imbibing or not. The true spirit is all about gathering and connecting. May these delicious spirit-free beverages lead you to more balanced ground.

There is a difference between making a drink without alcohol and crafting a delicious zero-proof beverage. One is just a drink that lacks alcohol; the other is a well-rounded, balanced, and tasty beverage. Make & Muddle mixers or infused simple syrups make all the difference.

Meet Cute Mocktail

Glass: Collins
Served: On the rocks
Yield: 1 drink

1 oz. Make & Muddle 2 Pepper Agave (or substitute; see chapter 4)
1 oz. lemon juice
Lemon seltzer
Long lemon twist
Sprig of rosemary for garnish

Spiral the lemon twist around the inside of a Collins glass, filling with ice as you go. Fill the glass halfway with seltzer. Add the agave and lemon juice and then fill up the glass with seltzer. Use a bar spoon or chopstick to stir the drink and position the lemon twist and rosemary sprig. Adjust the sweetness or tartness by adding more or less syrup or lemon juice.

> **"I firmly believe that there is a seat at the table for everyone whether they are imbibing or not."**

Cherry Fizz

Glass: Rocks
Served: On the rocks
Yield: 1 drink

1 oz. Make & Muddle Spiced Cherry Vanilla Syrup (or substitute; see chapter 4)
¼ oz. fresh lime juice
Lime seltzer
Lime wedge for garnish

Place the syrup and lime juice in a cocktail shaker full of ice and shake until cold. Strain into a rocks glass with ice. Top with lime-flavored seltzer. Garnish with a lime wedge.

Ruby Sue

Glass: Rocks
Served: On the rocks
Yield: 1 drink

1½ oz. brewed orange pekoe tea
1½ oz. Make & Muddle Orange Ginger Cranberry Shrub (or substitute; see chapter 4)
Dash grapefruit bitters
Lemon soda or seltzer to top
Orange twist or fresh cranberries for garnish

Build this drink in the glass. Stir together the tea, shrub, and bitters. Add ice, top with lemon soda, and stir gently. Garnish with an orange twist or a cocktail pick with fresh cranberries.

January Sour

Glass: Coupe
Served: Up
Yield: 1 drink

2½ oz. orange juice
1½ oz. brewed black tea
¾ oz. cinnamon simple syrup (see chapter 4)
½ oz. fresh lemon or lime juice
Dash cardamom bitters
Cherry or orange twist for garnish

Add the ingredients to a shaker with ice. Shake to combine. Double-strain into a chilled coupe glass. Garnish with a cherry or orange twist.

"May these delicious spirit-free beverages lead you to more balanced ground."

One of the best tropical cocktails is the Mondo Trasho. It tastes exactly like you expected a piña colada to taste until you actually ordered one and it was so sweet it made your teeth hurt. The spirit-free version is the Nondo Trasho. The viscosity of the coconut water adds a nice mouthfeel, and the froth from the pineapple juice (use fresh whenever possible) is awesome and can only be created by a good shake.

Nondo Trasho

Glass: Rocks
Served: On the rocks
Yield: 1 drink

3 oz. coconut water
1 oz. fresh pineapple juice
¾ oz. Make & Muddle 2 Pepper Agave (or substitute; see chapter 4)
¾ oz. fresh lime juice
1 bar spoon Make & Muddle 7 Syrup (or substitute; see chapter 4)

Add the ingredients to a shaker with ice and shake to combine. Dirty-dump the contents of the shaker (no straining) into the glass and enjoy. This drink is also great with a Tajín (a Mexican spice blend) rim.

BENEDICTION

At times, we have all had doubts about our abilities behind the bar. Maybe you didn't believe that you could mix a cocktail. Maybe you were intimidated by techniques and ingredients, barware and glassware. But a new day is dawning, my brothers and sisters, a day where a classic three-ingredient cocktail is in your heart at all times, a time when you can go out and spread the good news about booze. "For I am persuaded that neither death, nor life, nor angels, nor principalities, nor powers, nor things present, nor things to come, nor height, nor depth, nor any other creature, shall be able to separate us" from the good fellowship that happens over a good pour.

Therefore, my beloved brothers and sisters, be steadfast and immovable, be always abounding in the mixing of a great cocktail and the planning of a meaningful gathering, knowing that your labor is not in vain. This is our work throughout all generations, forever and ever. #cheersyall.

Acknowledgments

I began this book as an informal collection of recipes for my dearest friend, Beth. She is one of my fiercest champions, and our countless evenings on the porch, in front of the fire, or in the "think tank" (aka hot tub), laughing until we couldn't breathe, continue to be the genesis of great ideas and a guiding light in my life. Thank you, Beth, for being my chosen family. Thank you, Brent, for helping me become a better mixologist and for pushing me to aspire to be as good as you are at making magic happen in a glass. Your talent is, and has always been, an inspiration. Many thanks to Steven for being such a great sounding board and helping me navigate the murky waters of religion with clarity. Thank you to my momma. All my lofty ideals about good taste and my high standards for beautiful things came directly from you. I love you. Thank you to my family for always believing in me and supporting me, no matter how big or crazy my ideas are (even if we need to see what interest rates do in the new year). Thank you to the amazing team at the University Press of Kentucky for inspiring me to think bigger and helping me turn a lifelong dream into a reality. You made this cook and bartender an author. Thank you, Deborah Locker Group, for always being in my corner and for the magic you invoke wherever you go. Thank you to all my fellow cocktail evangelists and the faithful followers of Make & Muddle for believing in me and our company (especially Erin and Shannon). You are the driving force behind our innovation, our commitment to quality, and our exceptional cocktails. #cheersyall

BIBLIOGRAPHY

Biblical references on pages 101, 121, and 155 are drawn from the King James Version, Philippians 4:8, Proverbs 31:6-7, and Romans 8:38-39, respectively.

Burton, D. *The Raj at Table: A Culinary History of the British in India*. Faber & Faber, 1993.

Cawood, Clinton. "The Manhattan—Its History and Falsehoods." *Class Magazine*, February 2, 2023. https://classbarmag.com/news/fullstory.php/aid/915/The_Manhattan_-_its_history_and_falsehoods.html.

DeVito, Sophia. "Drink in History—The Hot Toddy." *Chilled Magazine*. https://chilledmagazine.com/drink-in-history-the-hot-toddy/.

Difford, Simon. "History of the Old Fashioned Cocktail." *Difford's Guide for Discerning Drinkers*. https://www.diffordsguide.com/g/1198/old-fashioned-cocktail/history.

———. "History of Sour Cocktails." *Difford's Guide for Discerning Drinkers*. https://www.diffordsguide.com/g/1133/sour-cocktails/history.

———. "Martini Cocktail and Its Evolution." *Difford's Guide for Discerning Drinkers*. https://www.diffordsguide.com/g/1121/martini/martini-history.

Schofield, J., and D. Schofield. *Schofield's Fine and Classic Cocktails: Celebrated Libations & Other Fancy Drinks*. Octopus, 2019.

Slaughter, Sam. "A Brief History of the Whiskey Sour Cocktail (and How to Make Different Versions)." *The Manual*, June 12, 2024. https://www.themanual.com/food-and-drink/brief-history-of-the-whiskey-sour/.

Sterling, Justine. "The Negroni: A Brief History." *Food & Wine Magazine*, November 15, 2022. https://www.foodandwine.com/cocktails-spirits/gin/brief-history-negroni.

INDEX

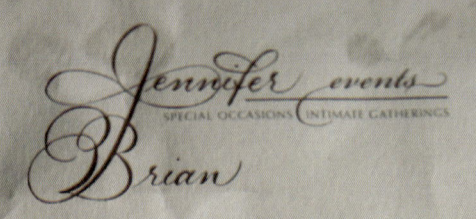

Boulevardier :

3 oz Bourbon (2)
1 oz Campari (1/2)
1 oz Sweet Vermouth (1)
DASH ORANGE Bitters

In a mixing glass with ice, combine
all ingredients & stir until cold. Strain into
a chilled cocktail glass or on the rocks.
Garnish w/orange peel.

Old Fashion :

3 oz. Bourbon
1/2 oz Simple Syrup
Healthy dash angostura bitters
Healthy dash orange Bitters
Orange Peel

1.5 bourbon
.75 aperol
3 coffee

2 C
1 B

Manhat	**Dbl Marg**
3 - bourbon	2:1 Teq to Dbl Coint
1 - verm	" Lime juice jalapeno
bitters	2 Gin — 2 sprigs lavender in std shaker
citrus	1 Germayne
	Top Seltzer — Chilled coupe 12 5 c seltzer
	½ Lemon juice — garnish c lavend

Whiskey Sour	Rosemary maple 3 oz Bourbon Sour
3 oz bourbon	1½ lemon
1.5 oz. Vanilla bourbon Simple Syrup	Dark amber 3/4 maple syrup
3/4 oz. Fresh lemon juice	Rosemary in shaker
Dash Bitters	& garnish c

- In a Shaker over ice. Garnish w/bourbon Cherry

Cosmo	1 teg
1 - Lime	2 gf juice
2 - cran	dash lemon bitters
1 - coin	
3 - vodka	1/8 2 pepper
	3/8 GGF